# 100 YEARS
# 100 LANDSCAPE
# DESIGNS

JOHN HILL

# 100 YEARS
# 100 LANDSCAPE
# DESIGNS

PRESTEL

MUNICH · LONDON · NEW YORK

# CONTENTS

# INTRODUCTION

*100 Years, 100 Landscape Designs* is a continuation of the experiment I started with *100 Years, 100 Buildings*. Like that book, this volume presents one hundred international projects completed in the past hundred years—one per year from 1917 to 2016. With each project accessible to the public, the goal is to present a list of one hundred must-visit places that span one hundred years and trace the evolution of various types of landscape designs. With the experience from my previous book, I knew the selection would balance icons and obscure gems with much in between, all the while giving me the opportunity to present important projects that did not meet the criteria of *100 Years, 100 Buildings*. It would be possible to include some landscape-oriented projects from the first book, but instead of repeating them I reference them in the text, where appropriate, and in the timeline.

As with buildings, my taste in landscape designs veers toward the modern. Although modern building caught on fairly quickly after being espoused by like-minded Europeans in the 1920s, modern landscape architecture took longer to establish itself. This delay can be attributed to the fact that buildings can be whitewashed in order to appear simple and mechanistic, but the main materials of landscapes—plants—are inherently complex and not pared down so easily. Further, modern architecture early on ascribed itself a role in addressing social issues through new forms, while landscape architecture was already concerned with social problems in the nineteenth century, yet in a Romantic style that persisted well into the next century. It wasn't until after World War II when prosperity and exuberance embraced modern landscape design that it became an important part of contemporary culture. My point here is that while *100 Years, 100 Buildings* traced the evolution of modern buildings exclusively, the projects in this book encompass traditional designs that are nevertheless significant and worth visiting.

### SELECTION CRITERIA

Being able to experience a landscape directly was one of the objective criteria I used in selecting the projects, although while all are publicly accessible, many places do charge admission fees. Other objective criteria included the fairly obvious facts that the projects are extant and are primarily exterior spaces. Since my previous book looks at structures that enclose interior spaces, *100 Years, 100 Landscape*

*Designs* heads outdoors to look at exterior spaces—places that put people in direct contact with nature. Therefore in terms of selection, I placed a higher merit on stand-alone projects: landscapes that are not secondary to buildings. Admittedly, many landscapes exist as companions to buildings, so this preference does not apply across the board, but it allowed me to make the often-tough decisions as to which landscape would "win out" in any given year.

Which takes us to the yearly format. It was tricky enough to nail down the precise dates of buildings in my previous book, but when it came to landscapes, "correct" dates were even cloudier. Which date is more important: start or completion? Is a landscape, something that grows and evolves over time, really ever complete? In response to these and other questions I determined a couple of guidelines that, with enough research, yielded the best dates but were flexible enough to apply to the two main types of landscapes—public and private—included in the book. So generally, *opening dates* are used for public projects that had "ribbon cuttings" or similar events to mark their openings. In some cases I used later dates: if, for instance, the project was completed in multiple phases. *Start dates* are used for gardens and other private landscapes, since typically those are ongoing projects that are worked on over decades with nary a goal of completion in mind. Even though these projects, to fit the criteria of this book, eventually opened to the public, it made sense to acknowledge their gestation.

Geographically, I strove to incorporate as many projects as possible outside the usual bastions of landscape design, but with my Western background the final list ended up with roughly 40 percent coming from Europe, 40 percent from North America, and the remaining 20 percent spread across Africa, Asia, Australia, and South America. Also, I tried not to repeat individual designers or firms, but sometimes that was futile, and in the process some notable names unfortunately ended up on the cutting-room floor: Thomas Church, Gertrude Jekyll, Shunmyō Masuno, Martha Schwartz, and SWA Group to name just a handful. Projects that did not make the cut but were strong contenders are listed in the timeline at the back of the book.

### TYPES OF LANDSCAPE DESIGNS

With my background in architecture and a strong interest in landscapes, my definition of landscape design embraces a wide range of types, not just gardens and parks. For me, landscape design is more than (just) the arrangement of plants; it is about shaping outdoor space for a particular purpose or function, and doing so in a way that is, for lack of a better term, poetic: defining a peculiar way of *being* within a natural environment. These types are described briefly as follows, listed from most to least numerous in these pages.

*Gardens and Parks*

Traditionally, gardens are the exclusive, private domains of individuals and families: cultivated landscapes that stand distinct from the "wild" nature beyond. Therefore gardens are staunchly dependent on their immediate surroundings, and the desire to control views beyond the footprints of gardens means many of them are the domains of the rich. Given this, the majority of gardens included in the book are older, historically important, and open to the public because of foundations that ensure their longevity—both of the gardens and their patrons' legacies. Parks, on the other hand, are inclusive, for everybody's use. They may use the same palette as gardens—plants, trees, water—but parks can range in size from less than an acre to thousands of acres. Parks are thus shaped by what land is available and what people will use them for. For centuries parks have been places of recreation, but today those uses are layered over ecological efforts (environmental remediation and habitat restoration) as well as economic benefits for public and private entities alike.

Two unique strains of landscape designs bridge these two types. *Botanical Gardens* are research institutions that collect plants and study them scientifically. They are sometimes similar in size to parks but often are laid out as a series of smaller gardens. In being open to the public, botanical gardens educate people about the value of nurturing landscapes and provide places for them to be in touch with nature. *Community Gardens* are found primarily in urban areas and exist to give people without yards the chance to grow flowers and vegetables on small parcels. Initially serving wartime needs, they are an increasingly popular means of obtaining fresh produce and teaching children about how food is grown.

*Land Art and Sculpture Parks*

Land art is a truly twentieth-century movement, although one that was short-lived. Starting in the late 1960s with earthworks by Robert Smithson and Michael Heizer, Land art was distinctly American, rooted in the expanses of the West. This means few people have laid eyes directly on artworks that have more to do with ancient landforms than the contemporary art world that embraced them. Although landscapes as settings for sculptures extend back to ancient civilizations, the proliferation of sculpture parks beginning in the late 1950s has made them a truly recent phenomenon because of the way they have impacted the production and consumption of art. As sculpture parks have expanded, so has the art—the bigger the better it seems, and better still when artworks engage with their settings as site-specific works. Sculpture parks benefit from the interaction of art and nature, and the best ones emphasize this dialogue over the individual elements.

*Plazas and Promenades*

These two types are dissimilar but united here by the importance of setting. Plazas are exclusively urban, situated on typically small lots in dense central business districts. More hard than soft, they traditionally catered to office workers on their lunch breaks, but have diversified recently in response to the changing demographics of cities. Promenades, on the other hand, can be located just about anywhere, though the ones I was drawn to forced designers to be creative in connecting points A and B: paths along and across rivers, on and beside historic hilltops, and even atop a double-decker highway.

*Campuses and Communities*

Campuses include both educational and corporate versions, and each works upon the same principle: buildings for shared use laid out on a large tract of land that functions for circulation and visual interest. Given the size of campuses, their landscape designs resemble parks, though with a strong integration of building and landscape. Like campuses, the integration of landscapes with buildings is important in communities, but so are the broader social and economic changes that they contend with directly. The new communities featured in this book are notable for defining ways of living on the land that are alternatives to the prevailing trends in cities and suburbs.

*Cemeteries and Memorials*

Grief is a process that benefits from nature, where the cycles of life and death are always visible. Many early cemeteries even functioned as parks; they were beautiful places that people would enjoy regardless of who was dwelling there. Modern cemeteries are not so well trodden, but they are more diverse in merging the facts of death with the abundance of nature. Memorials mark important historical events and are therefore truly public places for many people to gather and remember. Meaning is intentional with memorials more than any other type of landscape, and it is often found in their dialogues with urban and natural surroundings.

*Amphitheaters and Pools*

The last types covered in this book are recreational: one active and one passive. Amphitheaters, plain and simple, are gathering spaces for watching performances. A concert or other event is enhanced by an exterior setting, be it through trees and other natural features during the day or the stars at night. A public pool, though basically a place to swim, is more importantly a social space where this action takes place among friends and strangers. Like amphitheaters, pools are often found indoors, but the experience of swimming outdoors is made special through dramatic settings.

### MOVING FORWARD

What come to the fore in the above descriptions of landscape typologies are their settings: modern landscapes were and are about new settings. More than urban/suburban and rural/wild dichotomies, landscape designs must contend with loaded contexts: brownfields, historical sites, reclaimed land—no site is virgin and no site is without repercussions to the environment when developed and cultivated. Thankfully, it is rare to find landscape designers today who don't pepper their plans with native plants, for instance, or seriously address water, be it polluted groundwater, rising oceans, or depleted aquifers. Accordingly, landscape architects in the age of climate change and superstorms are overly ambitious and increasingly called on to save the world from the destructive excesses of automobiles, buildings, and industry.

"The New Landscape Declaration," written in 2016 by a group of landscape architects brought together by the Landscape Architecture Foundation (LAF), sums up the position. It came exactly fifty years after LAF's first "Declaration of Concern," which called for collaborative solutions to pollution, water shortages, and other crises. The new declaration asserts that the profession is ready to address this century's crises: rising seas, resource depletion, desertification, and species extinction. Although the problems have changed, the sentiment remains the same: losing contact with nature harms the environment and the human experience. Yet as the landscape professions confront our ecological crises, they can't just apply their expertise to technical solutions. Designers need to keep creating landscapes like the ones in this book: places that people can enjoy; places full of beauty and poetry; and ultimately places that cultivate humanity's role in nature.

# 1917 FILOLI

### Bruce Porter, Isabella Worn ▸ Woodside, California, United States

The westward view across the Sunken Garden and its lily pond ends in a distant ridge, a view that is protected by Filoli's many acres.

The Wedding Place, with its circular pool and lawn terraces, is tucked into one corner of the Walled Garden.

It is a rare treat to be able to visit a hundred-year-old estate and see it almost entirely in the same light as did its original residents. Such is the case with Filoli, the estate of entrepreneur William Bowers Bourn II, who ran the gold mine his father started and was also involved in water and power companies in the San Francisco area. His wealth enabled him to purchase 1,800 acres (728 hectares) in a valley near Crystal Springs Lake (his water company's reservoir), surrounded on three sides by a watershed that protected views of nature in all directions—and does so to this day.

Bourn hired San Francisco architect William Polk to design a forty-three-room mansion for him and his wife, Agnes, and they took up residence in 1917, anointing the estate Filoli after the credo, "Fight for a just cause, love your fellow man, live a good life." Bruce Porter (1865–1953) was responsible for the formal, English-style gardens: a scant 16 acres (6.5 hectares) of greenhouses, lawns, parterres, a sunken garden, and yew allée that were completed in 1927. The Bourns lived the good life on their Gilded Age estate until 1936, the year they both died. Since their only daughter had died ten years previous, the estate was put up for sale, bought by Lurline Matson Roth and William P. Roth, who lived there with their three children. Lurline had a strong hand in working the garden, but some continuity came from horticulturalist Isabella Worn (1869–1950), who worked with Porter on the original garden and came out of semiretirement to assist Lurline with existing and new gardens, the latter including a swimming pool. Bella, as she was known, had a busy career, marked by work on William Randolph Hearst's estate down the coast, but her passion is most evident at Filoli, which she worked on until her death at the age of eighty-one.

The Roths donated the house and gardens to the National Trust for Historic Preservation in the mid-1970s, providing an endowment for its maintenance. Visitors to Filoli today confront a series of roomlike gardens—the Knot Garden, Sunken Garden, and Walled Garden among them—walled by hedges or allées that embrace the people inside them much like the surrounding hills embrace the estate that was shaped by two families over the course of a half century.

# 1918 VILLANDRY

## Joachim Carvallo ▸ Touraine, France

Trimmed hedges frame flowers and vegetables throughout the gardens, a high-maintenance approach with aesthetically pleasing results.

The ornamental garden adjacent to the chateau is the early twentieth-century work of Sevillian artist Lozano with painter and landscape architect Javier de Winthuysen.

As mentioned in the introduction, it took a while for the architecture of landscapes in the twentieth century to be infused by modernism. Gabriel Guevrekian's cubist garden at Villa Noailles (see 1927) is seen as a watershed in this regard, but in the context of this book that leaves (at least) ten years of landscapes where tradition is strong. None is as immediately traditional as Villandry, whose gardens date back to 1532 and appear to be Renaissance creations in their entirety. In fact they are modern interpretations of four-hundred-year-old gardens, filtered through the imagination of Joachim Carvallo (1869–1936) between 1908 and 1918.

Carvallo, who studied science and medicine, married Ann Coleman, an American heiress whose 1906 inheritance enabled them to buy the dilapidated Château de Villandry, created as the sixteenth-century residence of France's minister of finance, Jean Le Breton, in the Loire Valley. At the time of purchase the gardens were the remnants of the handiwork of Marquis de Castellane, who saw the original Renaissance gardens as old-fashioned and therefore put in a romantic, English-style garden in the mid-1700s. Carvallo wanted to restore the gardens to their original glory to match the restored chateau, but, unlike the equally famous Château de Vaux-le-Vicomte, there was no surviving documentation of Villandry's Renaissance parquet. So, with his scientific background, he looked to the ground for hints and combined archaeological clues with sixteenth-century engravings by Jacques Androuet du Cerceau and other documents that gave him ideas as to the form of the Renaissance landscaping.

Carvallo's layout follows the surviving canals and the walled perimeter to define a number of geometrically precise areas on the 12-acre (4.8-hectare) trapezoidal property. Most prominent is the nine-square *potager* (kitchen garden), where smaller square, rectangular, cross-shaped, and even maze-shaped planting beds are filled with vegetables and boxed out by carefully trimmed shrubs. The ornamental gardens adjacent to the chateau are freer but no less precise in their geometries and high maintenance. Some creations, such as the herb garden and sun garden, were installed by Carvallo's heirs, who continue to preserve and develop the estate. In 2009 the gardens went 100 percent organic (no pesticides, only organic fertilizer, and traditional weeding), once again turning back the clock on this garden with traditional roots.

# 1919 THE HUNTINGTON BOTANICAL GARDENS

**William Hertrich** ▸ **San Marino, California, United States**

The native plants in the 10-acre (4-hectare) Desert Garden can tower over visitors; one cactus reportedly weighs in at 20 tons.

The 9-acre (3.6-hectare) Japanese Garden was born from a fascination with Asian culture that saw botanical gardens in Chicago, San Francisco, and St. Louis install their own versions.

Although the first botanical garden in the United States dates to 1730, in Philadelphia, they spread widely across the country in the nineteenth century, with notable gardens created in Chicago, New York, St. Louis, Washington, DC, and other cities. Not long after the turn of the century, industrialist Henry E. Huntington added to the list when he started to improve his 600-acre (243-hectare) tract overlooking the San Gabriel Valley near Los Angeles. Today the Huntington Library, Art Collections, and Botanical Gardens (its full name), founded in 1919 and opened to the public in 1928, has one of the preeminent botanical collections in any country.

Not many individuals would be able to turn their personal property into an impressive collection of gardens suitable for a botanical garden, but Huntington used his wealth and connections with factories, railways, and transportation to do things on a large scale. He set up an on-site nursery with over fifteen thousand plantings, installed a private spur track for unloading stone, and doubled a nearby reservoir for his needs. Of course Huntington didn't work alone: in 1904 he hired German horticulturalist William Hertrich (1878–1966) as superintendent, who worked on the gardens until his retirement in 1948, twenty-one years after his client's death. Working without a master plan, Hertrich pulled off one garden project after another. He started with the Lily Ponds and then worked with Huntington on the Palm, Desert, and Japanese gardens. The last was completed over the course of three months in 1912 as a gift for Huntington's second wife, with trees taken from other Huntington properties so as to look finished as early as possible.

The Japanese Garden, with its distinctive half-moon bridge, is a highlight of the Huntington Botanical Gardens, which now cover 120 acres (48.5 hectares) across more than a dozen distinct gardens. Another notable example is the Desert Garden, which Hertrich had to convince his client to install (cacti weren't appreciated then as they are now), and now features more than two thousand species of succulents and desert plants in sixty landscaped beds arranged by Hertrich for aesthetic affect rather than scientific classification. More than the other gardens, which highlight plants and styles from around the world, the Desert Garden celebrates the American Southwest and shows that its deserts are anything but barren wastelands.

# 1920 COLUMBUS PARK

## Jens Jensen ▸ Chicago, Illinois, United States

Columbus Park is one of only two open spaces in Chicago that is a National Historic Landmark—the other being Jensen's disciple Alfred Caldwell's Lily Pool (see 1938).

The "prairie river" lagoon at the heart of Columbus Park is fed by a series of waterfalls lined with stratified stone that was restored in the 1990s.

In terms of its open spaces, Chicago is known best for its 24 miles (39 kilometers) of parks and beaches kept "forever open, clear, and free" along Lake Michigan since the late 1800s. But what about parks for the throngs of residents living away from the lake, the primarily working-class families on the city's west side? The West Park System, made up of a trio of parks planned by William Le Baron Jenney and built under superintendent Jens Jensen (1860–1951) until 1900, addressed this deficiency. Twenty years later, Jensen realized his masterpiece at Columbus Park.

Born in Denmark, Jensen left for the United States in 1884 and ended up in Chicago the following year, when he was hired as a laborer for the West Parks. Promotions came quickly and by 1895 he was superintendent of one of the trio, Humboldt Park, but was let go five years later for political reasons. The prairie-style gardens he installed, which were made up of wildflowers collected from trips into the woods and prairie, were popular with the public, so he was reinstated as superintendent in 1906—this time for the whole West Park System—and was able to realize what he regarded as his most successful park, Columbus Park, on 135 acres (55 hectares) of farmland bordering suburban Oak Park.

Discovering what he thought was an ancient beach on the site, Jensen conceptualized Columbus Park as an interpretation of the state's native landscape. With a golf course already occupying the western half of the site, he placed a lagoon (present in each of the West Parks) on the eastern half, and from its excavation he created an elevated area with limestone waterfalls—the metaphorical spring that feeds the lagoon, which he called a "prairie river." To the east he also put in a natural swimming hole (now a typical Chicago Park District pool) and one of his signature council rings, where people can gather, tell stories, and put on performances.

Columbus Park was completed in 1920, the year Jensen stopped working for the City of Chicago permanently. Fifteen years later he closed his private practice downtown, moved to Wisconsin's Door County peninsula, and established the Clearing, a folk school that still operates. A testament to his standing, a *New York Times* obituary labeled Jensen "the dean of American landscape architecture."

# 1921 ÖSTRA KYRKOGÅRDEN

## Sigurd Lewerentz ▸ Malmö, Sweden

The pleached and pollarded linden trees on the cemetery's south half have an architectural quality that gives the walkways a rhythm and frames the graves.

In the middle of the second decade of the twentieth century, Swedish architect Sigurd Lewerentz (1885–1975) won two major competitions for cemeteries in his home country. In 1915, working with Erik Gunnar Asplund, he won the competition for the extension of Skogskyrkogården in south Stockholm (see *100 Years, 100 Buildings*), and one year later, working by himself, he won the competition to design Östra Kyrkogården (Eastern Cemetery) in Malmö, the city's largest cemetery, which was inaugurated on November 6, 1921. Lewerentz would devote six decades of his life to the project, which spanned from the beginning of his career to his very last building.

The title of his winning entry was "Ås," meaning "ridge," which arose from the natural feature running east-west across the 148-acre (60-hectare) site. Lewerentz initially placed the entrance at the east end of the site and provided a path along the ridge to give views of the cemetery's two halves: a grid of allées and dense plots to the south and a looser grid with verdant lawn and trees to the north. Shortly after the cemetery opened, the main path shifted to the south side of the ridge (a narrower path still follows the ridge), which mourners would reach after passing through a sunken ceremonial circle near the entrance. Lewerentz inserted a waiting room and the chapel of St. Birgitta, both in his then-Neoclassical style, into the side of the ridge. The chapel pointed mourners to the south and to an allée of linden trees, the next path in the cemetery's procession of grief.

Lewerentz added a number of structures to the cemetery in the decades following its opening. Most important were a crematorium in 1931 (no longer in use), the chapels of St. Gertrude and St. Knut appending it in 1943, and a bell tower in the same year. All these structures exhibit the architect's more personal style that followed his neoclassical origins; more important they are located toward the west end of the site. A gravitational shift in this direction was made official with Lewerentz's 1969 flower kiosk (his last building anywhere) and the relocation of the entrance to the adjacent west gate. More than just a beautiful setting for a collection of some of the architect's best buildings, the landscape Lewerentz designed has a quiet grace that holds its own with the masterpiece he realized with Asplund in Stockholm.

# 1922 GIARDINO DI NINFA

## Caetani family ▸ Sermoneta, Italy

The ruins and the plantings work together to create a romantic landscape that is as much about Italy as it is about the Caetani family.

The wooden bridge is one of three structures traversing the stream that cuts the garden into two halves.

Unlike buildings, which are only prey to the occasional renovation or addition, landscapes are ever-changing, unstable entities. With trees, shrubs, plants, flowers, and other vegetation shaping their spaces, gardens in particular are at the mercy of nature and the wills of those tending to them. The Giardino di Ninfa (Garden of Ninfa), about 50 miles (80 kilometers) southeast of Rome, is a prime example of time's role in a garden's evolution, considering it was developed upon centuries-old ruins and is the result of the work of three generations of the family that owned the land.

The Caetani family could trace itself from some time in the ninth century until 1977, when Lelia Caetani, the last daughter, died. The land that she gardened was acquired in the fourteenth century by Boniface Caetani, who obtained the papal fiefdom of Ninfa and other nearby estates. Regardless of wars, pillaging, and other conflicts levied on the land, Ninfa stayed in the family until its end. It was in 1922 when the story of the Garden of Ninfa began, when English-born Ada Wilbraham, mother of Gelasio Caetani, planted the roses that still grow over the ruin's stone walls. Gelasio restored some of the buildings and planted cypresses, cedars, and walnut trees. After Gelasio's death, Marguerite, the wife of his brother Roffredo, added flowering trees but, more notably, also added more streams to the site. Lastly, their daughter Lelia, an artist, followed the principles laid down by the previous generations and positioned trees and plants in an artistic manner, selecting them primarily for visual effect. She shaped greatly what visitors see today and ensured the garden's longevity through the creation of the Fondazione Roffredo Caetani in 1972.

The 20-acre (8-hectare) garden sits among a 350-acre (141-hectare) wildlife refuge, where the whole is a lush landscape thanks to good soil, warm breezes from the south, mountains shielding cold northern winds, and springs yielding fresh water throughout the site. Visitors navigating the informally laid-out landscape come across three bridges that traverse a spring-fed stream, while they also encounter numerous churches and other buildings in restored or ruined states. The last—the ruins—give the garden the almost legendary romantic character that transports visitors to another time.

# 1923 JARDIN MAJORELLE

## Jacques Majorelle ▸ Marrakech, Morocco

Jacques Majorelle's house and studio, which since 2011 houses a museum of Berber culture, is a striking backdrop to the garden's large cacti.

Color extends from the house and studio into all parts of the garden, covering most of the hard surfaces and accentuating the green plants throughout.

Gardening and painting are two artistic fields that are often found to be synergistic. With the earth as the canvas and plants and flowers as paints, a garden can be like a living painting in the mind of a painter. Jardin Majorelle, named for its creator, French painter Jacques Majorelle (1886–1962) exudes this marriage of painting and nature through its combination of exotic vegetation and colorful surfaces.

The only son of furniture designer and École de Nancy founder Louis Majorelle, whose designs were rooted in natural forms, Jacques was brought up with a fascination for nature, particularly plant forms. He studied architecture and painting, but in 1917, unable to serve in World War I due to health issues, he visited Morocco and fell in love with Marrakech. The "Ochre City" served as his home base for exploring the rest of the country and from 1923, when he bought a 4-acre (1.6-hectare) plot on the border of a palm grove, until near his last days it would be his permanent home. On a trip to the Atlas Mountains he was enamored with the Berber tribes, who painted parts of their houses an eye-catching cobalt blue. Back in Marrakech he built a house and studio designed by Paul Sinoir that was inspired by the Berber towers, its walls covered with a paint color that came to be known as Majorelle blue. Majorelle planted the garden with plants and trees collected from his travels and treated the garden's hard surfaces with the same painterly attention as the house and studio. He opened his creation to the public in 1947 and in 1980 Yves Saint-Laurent and Pierre Bergé, who shared Majorelle's love of Morocco, bought it and then maintained and expanded on his vision.

Visitors to Jardin Majorelle encounter a garden only about half the size it was in Majorelle's day, but one that is dense with cacti, bamboo, and other plantings from the tenures of both owners. Bright-red paths lined with Majorelle-blue planters wind throughout the planted areas that are maintained by a system of irrigation canals rooted in traditional Moroccan techniques. Water is also found in a tile fountain near the entrance, a lily pool, and a fountain fronting the house and studio. These elements reiterate the garden's oasis-like character in the desert city, as well as the infiltration of color in nearly every surface of the painter's garden.

# TUINEN MIEN RUYS

### Mien Ruys ▸ Dedemsvaart, Netherlands

Mien Ruys's predilection for modern forms and arrangements within her gardens is apparent in this view highlighting some perennial borders.

Her first garden—the Wild Garden, with its small square pool—survives to this day, nearly one hundred years after being realized.

Just as architects build houses for themselves as a way of experimenting with new forms and materials, landscape architects do the same with home gardens. Without any options for a design education in her native Netherlands, in 1924 at the age of just nineteen Mien Ruys (1904–1999) took the initiative and began experimenting on some land near her parents' property in the town of Dedemsvaart. (Her father owned a nursery, so she knew of her chosen career early in life and was able to put it into practice before receiving an education.) She would use the gardens as a testing ground for her ideas for more than seventy years.

Eventually Ruys studied landscape architecture in Berlin, in the 1930s, but before that she had created a few gardens of her own in Dedemsvaart. First was the Wild Garden, for which she dug a small pond and surrounded it with plantings, learning the hard way which ones would survive in the shade and in acidic soil. After meeting English gardener Gertrude Jekyll, a client of her father, she embarked upon the Perennial Border; this was the first Jekyll-style mixed border in Holland and was therefore highly influential. Ruys's strong talents born partly from her willingness to take risks and learn from them meant she was a significant influence throughout her career—which was prolific, with more than three thousand projects to her name. Sometimes her impact on fellow landscape designers was for the worse rather than better: she earned the nickname *bielzen* (sleeper) for her early use of railroad ties, though she regretted their widespread popularity and was known to have lamented, "What have I done?" The Marsh Garden, the last of her thirty experimental gardens at home, is perhaps a reaction to her nickname, though it's also a sign of her ecological thinking veiled behind the modern forms of her gardens: ashamed of so much wood from rain forests being used in construction, she explored the use of recycled plastic for pathways and steps over water.

Tuinen Mien Ruys (*tuinen* is Dutch for "gardens") has been managed by the Mien Ruys Garden Foundation since 1976. The foundation allows the public to access the gardens and carries on its namesake designer's belief in experimentation through the installation of new gardens and new layouts for existing gardens. Ruys would be happy.

# 1925 THIJSSE'S HOF

### Jacobus Pieter Thijsse, Leonard Springer ▸ Bloemendaal, Netherlands

A life-size statue of Jacobus Pieter Thijsse looks out across the landscape that embodies the lifelong principles he espoused in the Netherlands.

A path cuts through the woodlands where Thijsse attempted to grow species of dune flora as documented in F. W. van Eeden's *Weeds*, published in 1886.

Over the course of the first fifty years of J. P. Thijsse's (1865–1945) life, the Netherlands' population doubled to seven million, which led to the despoliation of the countryside, a loss of natural resources, and a lack of ready access to nature for those in overcrowded cities like Amsterdam, where he lived before moving to Bloemendaal. Thijsse trained and worked as a teacher but his interests veered toward biology. He combined the two in his devotion to protecting nature and educating the public about its value.

Among his many undertakings—forming environmental laws, setting up nature conservation organizations, working on the Boschplan (Amsterdam Development Plan), taking groups of schoolchildren on nature walks around the city, and writing books on Dutch butterflies, birds, and flowers—Thijsse conceived the idea of so-called instructive parks. He envisioned each town would have its own 5-acre (2-hectare) park where students would experience nature on regular visits, with larger cities like Amsterdam and Rotterdam having closer to a dozen such areas. The prototype was Thijsse's Hof (*hof* translates as "court") in Bloemendaal, near the sea and west of Amsterdam, on land donated by the local government in 1925 to celebrate the town's famous resident's sixtieth birthday. There Thijsse developed a plant and bird garden that would contain all the plants that grew in the sand dunes of the town's Kennemerland region, to teach visitors about the dunes and aid in their conservation.

Thijsse turned to landscape architect Leonard Springer (1855–1940) to lay out the 5-acre garden on land that formerly served as a potato field and was spared from nearby development in the early 1920s. Most of the garden is contained by a perimeter of dune forest created from oak coppice, where the trees were cut back periodically to stimulate growth. In the center of the garden is a pond, and in between it and the forest are grasslands, a slope with roses, and a thicket dominated by shrubs with berries. The last, as part of the garden's approximately four hundred species of plants, aids in attracting around twenty-four species of birds to the gardens.

In 1995 a statue of Thijsse by sculptor Jolanda Prinsen was added to the garden, and in 2015 a pavilion designed by Dirk Vlaar of BBHD opened at the entrance to the garden. The latter helps accommodate the hundreds of schoolchildren who visit annually and extend Thijsse's goals of education and conservation.

# 1926 NAUMKEAG

## Fletcher Steele ▸ Stockbridge, Massachusetts, United States

The famous Blue Steps are flanked by birch trees and highlighted by curved white railings that stand out against clipped hedges.

The lines of the Rose Garden's rose-graveled paths punctuated by floribunda roses do from above what the Blue Steps do from the front.

A forty-four-room "cottage" designed by Stanford White of McKim, Mead & White in 1885 for the family of lawyer and ambassador Joseph Hodges Choate anchors the 48-acre (19-hectare) property known as Naumkeag—the Indian name for Salem, Massachusetts. Yet it is the 8 acres (3.2 hectares) of formal gardens near the house that have made it one of the most recognizable estates in the American Northeast.

Choate employed landscape architect Nathan F. Barrett (1845–1919) to lay out a two-tier garden highlighted by an evergreen allée. Joseph, his wife, and their five children picnicked, played tennis and golf, and hosted parties on the landscaped grounds, but when daughter Mabel inherited the estate she oversaw a redesign with landscape architect Fletcher Steele (1885–1971). Mabel hired Steele in 1926, when he started with the service court. Their fruitful collaboration lasted nearly thirty years, such that Steele had his own bedroom upstairs. He eventually designed a handful of garden "rooms," each one formally distinct and eclectic in its design elements.

The first garden chronologically, the Afternoon Garden, was inspired by Mabel's appreciation of outdoor rooms in California, though Steele responded with a design that recalls the Mediterranean: finial-capped gondola posts dredged from Boston Harbor define two sides of the space and frame views of the distant hills. Next came the adjacent South Lawn, considered the first modern earthwork; Steele used demolition fill from a nearby construction site to form a meandering berm (raised border) that culminates in a cast-iron pagoda. The Chinese Garden on the north side of the house followed as an outpost for artifacts Choate brought back from her trip to China. The Blue Steps, completed in 1938, came next, and are the most recognizable part of the gardens. They started out as a request for simple steps to connect the house to the clipping garden down the hill on the west, but Steele gave Choate a cascading fountain flanked by steps and landings for her to rest on her ascent. He then designed the Rose Garden, with sinuous pathways meant to be seen from Mabel's bedroom window, and then finished his work in 1955 with a wall and Moon Gate for the Chinese Garden, three years before Mabel died. Fortunately for fans of garden art, she left the house and its 48 acres to the Trustees of Reservations, which completed an extensive, multiphase restoration in the summer of 2016.

# 1927 VILLA NOAILLES

**Gabriel Guevrekian** ▸ **Hyères, France**

Although designed as a stable, ready-made garden less dependent on the growth of plants than other gardens, the small triangle of land has changed and been restored numerous times since its completion; the latest restoration took place in 2016.

Held in 1925 on both banks of the Seine in Paris, the Exposition Internationale des Arts Décoratifs was a vastly influential world's fair that spread art deco and other modern styles throughout the world. It played host to what is widely considered the very first avant-garde garden, Gabriel Guevrekian's (1900–1970) cubist-inspired Jardin d'Eau et de Lumiere (Garden of Water and Light). Although it occupied just a tiny triangular site, the garden made a big impression on many, including Charles de Noailles, who commissioned Guevrekian to design a similar garden for a house he was building on the French Riviera. The Garden of Water and Light is long gone, but the garden at Villa Noailles (now an arts center and exhibition space) remains, making it the earliest cubist garden that people can still experience.

De Noailles was an enthusiastic collector of modern art, so it made sense that he consulted the most forward-thinking architects at the time to design the villa for him and his wife, Marie-Laure. These included Le Corbusier and Ludwig Mies van der Rohe, but in the end he hired Parisian architect Robert Mallet-Stevens to design the huge 19,000-square-foot (1,800-square-meter) house terracing up the Hyères hillside. The architect might have a street named for him in Paris's 16th arrondissement, where five of his urban villas congregate, but in history books Guevrekian's miniscule garden overshadows the grand modern house it's attached to.

The garden is located on a triangular plot at the house's southeastern corner. It backs up against the house on one side and is defined by plain white walls on the other two sides. It juts from the house like the prow of a ship angled toward the Mediterranean, which is visible over the stepped walls at the garden's far corner. Here Guevrekian placed a rotating sculpture by Jacques Lipchitz (since removed) that was framed by two orange trees. An alternating grid of pavers and plantings, with triangular sections close to the wall, ascends gently toward the far corner, where all the lines of the garden converge. Yet this is not a garden to be experienced from within. Rather it is one to be viewed from the house itself, particularly from the roof terrace that overlooks it through two square openings cut into a tall parapet. From here, the garden is a pure abstraction of lines, shapes, and colors.

# 1928 SUNNYSIDE GARDENS

## Clarence S. Stein and Henry Wright, Marjorie Sewell Cautley
## New York City, United States

The most distinctive aspect of Sunnyside Gardens' layout is the pedestrian paths that cut across the blocks and provide residents access to the communal open spaces in the middle of the blocks.

Three years after completing Sunnyside Gardens, Clarence S. Stein and Henry Wright built the Phipps Garden Apartments, whose buildings and courtyards are included in the historic district.

At the end of the nineteenth century, Ebenezer Howard founded the garden city movement in England as an antidote to industrialization and urbanization; planned communities were envisioned to sit in the countryside with balanced and separated areas for living, working, and recreation. Two "new towns" following the movement's principles were built in the first two decades of the twentieth century, but it wasn't until the late 1920s that the United States would see its first version of the garden city—only four miles from the skyscrapers of Midtown Manhattan.

Planners, architects, and partners Clarence S. Stein (1882–1975) and Henry Wright (1878–1936) were the visionaries behind Sunnyside Gardens, located on 53 acres (21 hectares) of undeveloped land in Sunnyside, Queens, next to a rail yard but close to public transportation. Stein returned from his travels in England after World War I as a disciple of Howard and of Raymond Unwin, the architect of one of the new towns. Stein and Wright cofounded the Regional Planning Association of America (RPAA) in 1923 and soon after convinced developer and RPAA officer Alexander M. Bing to build a garden city. Practicalities pointed to a pilot of sorts within the confines of New York rather than a completely new town, so Bing's newly founded City Housing Corporation bought the land in 1924 and four years later 1,202 units of housing in more than 600 buildings were completed on sixteen full and partial blocks.

The innovations of Sunnyside Gardens started with the housing units themselves and extended to their arrangements on the long, north-south blocks and the network of pedestrian paths between buildings. Each of the units—row houses and apartment buildings designed by architect Frederick L. Ackerman—was shallow, with small front yards and generous backyards. These buildings were first placed along the street, but later turned perpendicular to the street; in either case communal areas were provided in the middle of the blocks and pedestrian paths cut east-west across the blocks to provide access to their centers. The success of these open spaces is due in part to the site planning but also to the work of landscape architect Marjorie Sewell Cautley (1891–1954), who designed the landscaping to complement the brick buildings while also giving residents distinct places to exercise, congregate, and relax. The success of the whole undertaking is evident in Sunnyside Gardens being named a New York City historic district in 2007.

# 1929 LADEW TOPIARY GARDENS

## Harvey Smith Ladew II ▸ Monkton, Maryland, United States

Harvey Smith Ladew II was described as a "gardener, sporting art patron and good companion" by an English society magazine, something his Hunt Scene captures perfectly.

The gardens north of the house extend out along a 1,000-foot (305-meter) axis past topiary obelisks and an oval pool.

Topiary—the artistic clipping of trees or shrubs into ornamental shapes—traces its existence back to the Roman Empire, as documented by Pliny the Elder in his thirty-seven-volume *Historia Naturalis* in 79 AD. Then, as later, boxwood and yews were manicured to express the personality of the owner, be it a Roman or a millionaire living on the East Coast of the United States; Harvey Smith Ladew II (1887–1976) is an example of the latter. Starting in 1929, he maintained one of the most distinctive topiary creations of any place at any time.

Ladew was born into privilege in New York, a situation that stemmed from his grandfather's leather business. He served in World War I, but immediately following it he started spending his winters in England, feeding his passion for horses and fox hunting and discovering an appreciation for topiary. Fox hunting was more difficult back home on Long Island, which was getting crowded with suburban sprawl. So in late 1929 Ladew bought a farm with more than 200 acres (81 hectares) near Baltimore—a convenient location, since it bordered the Elkridge Harford Hunt Club. The farmhouse that would serve as the club's first headquarters needed immediate attention, so he added wings, redid the interiors, renovated the outbuildings, and then set aside 22 acres (9 hectares) next to the house for formal gardens that he would lay out and shape until the outbreak of World War II. In 1971, with a nonprofit set up to maintain the gardens, his creation opened to the public.

Today, visitors to Ladew Topiary Gardens first encounter the Hunt Scene: a fox, hounds, and a Ladew-esque sportsman on a horse jumping over a fence. Impatient with the European tradition of training young shrubs, he used wire frames to train and trim large shrubs to get immediate results. Although this is the most famous scene at Ladew, the rest of the gardens are full of pleasant surprises, topiary and otherwise. Boxwood, privet, hemlock, and yews exist in the form of unicorns, sea horses, butterflies, and obelisks, while a number of gardens harken back to English traditions, particularly the White Garden, which was modeled on the garden of the same name at Sissinghurst Castle Garden (see 1930). A Nature Walk was added in 1999 as a contrast to the manicured gardens and as a means of getting people to explore on foot what Ladew traversed on horseback long ago.

# 1930 SISSINGHURST CASTLE GARDEN

## Vita Sackville-West, Harold Nicolson ▸ Kent, England

The view from the tower with the Rondel in the middle of the Rose Garden at right and the South Cottage at left; the brick wall extending from the cottage into the lower-right corner hints at the once-larger extents of the medieval buildings.

Vita Sackville-West called the world-famous White Garden, seen here with the tower in the distance, her "grey, green and white garden" in recognition of the foliage needed to make the white flowers pop.

Few gardens are wholly original creations. Most exhibit layouts and planting designs that follow from gardens that came before, be they from the recent past or long ago. Sissinghurst Castle Garden, the creation of husband-and-wife diplomat Harold Nicolson (1886–1968) and author Vita Sackville-West (1892–1962), was influenced by notable British designers, but it was executed so well that it became as influential in its own right.

The 450-acre (182-hectare) estate they purchased in early 1930 dates back to the Middle Ages, when it was occupied by a large manor house surrounded by a moat. In the sixteenth century the house was expanded by Sir John Baker and his son, the latter turning it into a hunting lodge where he hosted Queen Elizabeth I. Subsequently a war prison and a farm, the impressive courtyard buildings were damaged by a fire in the late 1700s, so only the Tower and South Cottage were intact when the couple took over in 1930. Sackville-West was particularly drawn to the ruined nature of the site (still a working farm at the time), especially the fairy-tale-like Tower, where she eventually put her writing room. Before dealing with the buildings or interiors, they started cleaning and clearing the site to create the garden on 5 acres (2 hectares) adjacent to the buildings and brick-walled ruins. The self-taught, creative couple was influenced by, among other British landscape designers, the joint creations of architect Edwin Lutyens and garden designer Gertrude Jekyll. Nicolson first laid out a handful of Lutyens-esque axial vistas across the irregular site and a series of outdoor "rooms," such as the Rondel, bordered by clipped hedges, and Sackville-West followed with her abundant, colorful plantings inspired by Jekyll's informal techniques.

Sackville-West's plantings, further influenced by gardener William Robinson, were characteristically exuberant, with a full range of plants mixed up in borders yet following particular themes. Her ideas about color led to three main gardens: the White Garden, the Purple Border, and the sunset-colored Cottage Garden. Most famous and influential among these is the White Garden, an experiment whose success is witnessed in numerous imitations since (see 1929). The couple eagerly shared their creation, first opening the garden to the public in 1938. Following Sackville-West's death in 1962, Sissinghurst was given to the National Trust, which has maintained it and kept it open to the public since 1967.

# 1931 INNISFREE GARDEN

## Walter Beck, Lester Collins ▸ Millbrook, New York, United States

The Middle Terrace, with its mixings of plantings and rocks, sits close to the location of the original mansion.

The Point, with its three signature rocks, juts into Tyrrel Lake toward the garden's Pine Island in the distance.

Named after the 1888 W. B. Yeats poem "The Lake Isle of Innisfree," the 200-acre (81-hectare) Innisfree Garden is located about 90 miles (145 kilometers) north of New York City. Designed by two men at different times over the course of more than sixty years, the garden is rooted in Chinese garden designs but exudes its own distinctive charms.

In 1922 artist Walter Beck (1864–1954), the first man in the Innisfree story, married Marion Burt Stone, the daughter of Wellington R. Burt, a wealthy lumber baron. The newlyweds decided to build a Queen Anne–style home on her 950 acres (384 hectares) in Dutchess County, New York, to be accompanied eventually by an English garden. But in 1930 Beck had an itch for the garden to be something different, and during a yearlong trip to London he discovered the answer in an eighth-century scroll painting by Chinese painter, poet, and gardener Wang Wei. He noticed the gardens had enclosures like the sides of a cup and was determined to re-create the effect next to their mansion. So from their return to Millbrook until his death, Beck created a number of distinct, three-dimensional compositions made of rocks from the site and plantings with the help of his wife, but it wasn't until after his death that the cup gardens came together into a whole.

Shortly after Beck's death, his widow hired landscape architect Lester Collins (1914–1993), a student of Japanese gardens whom the couple met in 1938, to plan out the future of Innisfree, which opened to the public in 1960, one year after Marion died. In 1972, 750 acres (303 hectares) were sold to Rockefeller University for a field research center and in 1982 the incompatible mansion was razed; the remaining land is devoted to the gardens and is surrounded by a buffer of trees. From the opening until his death, Collins doubled the size of the gardens that Beck had created, while simultaneously simplifying the plantings from high- to low-maintenance to fit the Innisfree Foundation's small budget. He created new paths between Beck's cup gardens and shaped the land to create new gardens that stay true to Beck's Eastern influences. A visit to Innisfree Garden today is a meandering counterclockwise circuit around 40-acre (16-hectare) Tyrrel Lake, which serves as a quiet backdrop for many of the cup gardens encountered along the way.

# 1932 PROMENADE ALONG THE EMBANKMENTS AND BRIDGES OF THE LJUBLJANICA RIVER

## Jože Plečnik ▸ Ljubljana, Slovenia

The Triple Bridge includes stairs down to lower-level walkways that unfortunately were not realized in full.

Jože Plečnik planted willow trees along the stretch of the promenade between the Triple Bridge and the Cobbler's Bridge, seen here in the distance.

One of the earliest and most influential texts on urban planning is Camillo Sitte's 1889 book, *City Planning According to Artistic Principles*, in which the Austrian architect and theoretician argued for, among other things, well-considered urban spaces over grand vistas that prioritized the movement of traffic. Although directed at his native Vienna, Sitte applied the book's principles to Ljubljana in a town-planning competition following an earthquake that hit the city in 1895. Sitte would not realize anything in Ljubljana, but his ideas informed the designs that Jože Plečnik (1872–1957), who worked in Vienna and Prague and returned to his native city in 1921, would carry out there in the following decades.

Plečnik realized notable public buildings in Ljubljana in this time, including the National and University Library (see *100 Years, 100 Buildings*), but he also focused his efforts on the city's public spaces, most notably along and over the Ljubljanica River, which separated the old town on the east from newer developments on the west. Work had started in 1913 on reconstructing the river's banks out of concrete, but when Plečnik took over around 1928 the city adopted his more artistic approach, which would turn the waterway into a pedestrian spine and civic amenity with new buildings, public spaces, and promenades. He proposed no less than three bridges traversing the river, most famously the Triple Bridge, a reworking of an existing bridge where he added two new pedestrian crossings on either side and sheathed the whole in stone balustrades. Both the Triple Bridge and the pedestrian Cobbler's Bridge to the south were completed in 1932, connected to each other by promenades at street level that today are lined by restaurants with outdoor seating, much like the San Antonio River Walk (see 1946). Another prominent piece is the Central Market, which abuts the river directly north of the Triple Bridge.

The extent of Plečnik's work along the Ljubljanica River totals nearly 1.5 miles (2.4 kilometers), from crossings over the Gradaščica River on the south to the sluice gate north of the Triple Bridge. Upon the realization this century that traffic and parking had taken over most of Plečnik's river interventions, the city carried out extensive renovations that reinvigorated the spirit of the original. Plečnik's belief in his city as a work of art has translated into a city that refers to itself in some places as "Plečnik's Ljubljana."

# 1933 AARHUS UNIVERSITY

## Christian Frederik Møller, Carl Theodor Sørensen ▸ Aarhus, Denmark

The ponds at the center of the campus give it the feeling of a park rather than that of a traditional academic institution.

An amphitheater, the most famous landscape element on the campus, and ivy-covered retaining wall navigate the dramatic change in elevation at the north end of the site.

Oxford and Cambridge, two of the oldest universities, have influenced much of modern higher education, including the layouts of campuses—individual colleges articulated as buildings forming green quadrangles. One would be hard-pressed to mistake Aarhus University with these two schools, but with brick buildings surrounding a landscape of ponds, lawns, and oak trees, the English roots of campus design are still in evidence.

Aarhus University was founded in 1928 and the following year was given a hilly piece of land cut by a ravine north of the city center for its 30-acre (12-hectare) campus. Architect C. F. Møller (1898–1988), with Kay Fisker and Povl Stegmann, and landscape architect C. Th. Sørensen (1893–1979), won the 1931 competition for the campus with a free grouping of buildings arranged about an open valley with ponds formed by damming the brook at the north end of the site. Although they won the competition outright, criticism of the design followed, most notably from Denmark's King Christian X, who disliked the modern flat roofs (Fisker and Stegmann withdrew from the project following these comments) and urged Møller to find inspiration in the traditional Danish manor. The architect complied, and the resulting simple block buildings with yellow-brick walls and shallow gable roofs quietly merge with the landscape to give the university its identity.

Before the opening of the university's first buildings in 1933, criticism of the landscape design was levied at the use of a single species of tree: oak, rather than beech, Denmark's national tree. For Sørensen, oak was a symbol of the country's roots, since the species dates back to Denmark's Bronze Age, and from a practical perspective oaks would have a better chance of thriving alongside the buildings. It took a while for the landscape to catch up with the buildings, though, since all the oaks were planted as acorns—the creation of the campus became a symbol of the creation of a new university. As the university expanded over the years (now it covers 53 acres, or 21 hectares), it called on Møller and the eponymous successor firm, so the campus maintained its appearance as university leaders came and went. Even though Sørensen was removed from the project in its early years (Møller kept him on covertly), a few years before his death he admitted to it being the project that brought him the greatest happiness.

# 1934 OBSERVATORIELUNDEN

### Erik Gunnar Asplund ▸ Stockholm, Sweden

A rocky area on the side of Observatoriekullen gives the impression that the hill is the source of the pool's water.

The shallow pool and willow trees perfectly frame the orange drum of Erik Gunnar Asplund's Stockholm Stadsbiblioteket.

Erik Gunnar Asplund (1885–1940), together with Sigurd Lewerentz, was responsible for Skogskyrkogården, one of the most widely hailed landscapes between the two World Wars. Their design for that cemetery extension is included in *100 Years, 100 Buildings*, but Lewerentz's Östra Kyrkogården (see 1921 in this volume), also a cemetery, and Asplund's design for the park beside his Stockholm Stadsbiblioteket (Stockholm Public Library) in the center of the city's Vasastaden district make it clear that the two architects had strong interests in, and were extremely capable at, shaping landscapes.

The park Asplund designed next to the Stadsbiblioteket was completed in 1934, six years after the completion of the library, with its distinctive cylindrical rotunda and brown (now orange) exterior. The most well-regarded architect in Sweden at the time, Asplund was hired in 1918 to set up a competition for the building, but the committee warmed to him and decided to commission him directly. He sited the library at the north end of a large block dominated by the Observatoriekullen (Observatory Hill), which was preserved as a park in his design for the adjacent Observatorielunden. With the library set back from the corner of Odengatan and Sveavägen Streets, and with the main entrance and retail space facing the latter, some land was set aside for a new park south of the library and east of the hill. In 1924 Asplund capably won a competition for the park with a design that frames his library and the rocky hill, which the wider area resembled before being leveled for development.

Asplund's simple, straightforward park design places a large, shallow rectangular pool parallel to Sveavägen. Willows surround the pool and benches in front of a low wall along the sidewalk offer views toward the library and hill. On the other side of the pool is a lawn sloping up to the hill, which is also the source of the pool's water. Here, Asplund crafted some *rus in urbe*: what looks like a winding mountain stream with boulders is in fact an artificial stream made to appear as if it is bursting from the hill. The importance of the hill is reiterated in the library's plan; Asplund angled the building slightly toward it. More important, though, is the link between Asplund's library and his park, a link that should be strengthened when restorations to both being carried out at the time of writing are complete.

# 1935 JUBILEE POOL

## Captain F. Latham ▸ Penzance, England

The triangular pool that juts into the sea on a rocky peninsula consists of a huge adult pool and a smaller children's pool in one corner.

In the interwar years in Europe, lidos—open-air swimming pools—were popular fixtures in parks, with the United Kingdom building close to fifty of them in the 1930s. Most were located in London, giving city dwellers some recreation in summer months, though, all told, less than a dozen were still in use at the end of the century. The Jubilee Pool in Cornwall, near the western tip of England, is one of the few lidos from this period still in use today (and one of only a handful of saltwater tidal pools in use in Europe—see also 1966), thanks in part to a local community proud of the pool's streamlined, cubist-inspired design.

The Jubilee Pool opened in May 1935 to celebrate the silver jubilee of King George V, the same year the seaside De La Warr Pavilion, designed by Erich Mendelsohn and Serge Chermayeff, opened in East Sussex (see *100 Years, 100 Buildings*) with its own streamlined design. Captain F. Latham is not as familiar a name as Mendelsohn and Chermayeff, but that is because—as was common in lidos at the time—the borough engineer was responsible for the design of Jubilee Pool. In this role Latham sited the pool on a piece of land jutting southward into the sea, a traditional bathing spot in Penzance. He employed a triangular footprint with undulating walls to combat against the sometimes-fierce waves of the Cornish seas and protect visitors from strong winds. Between these outer walls and the inner walls of the triangular pool was a raised terrace wide enough for sunbathing, picnicking, watching swimmers in the large pool below, or even taking in the occasional concert.

Latham's design held up well until the 1970s when the pool was prey to a couple of decades of neglect. By the early 1990s it was looking dilapidated and a proposal to cover the pool was offered. John Clarke, a local retired architect, found merit in its original design and formed the Jubilee Pool Association to gain the pool a Grade Two landmark listing and raise funds for its restoration. All was well again after it reopened in 1994, until freak winter storms ten years later caused serious structural damage. Extensive repairs were made and the pool reopened in May 2016, eighty-one years after it first opened in celebration of royalty. Now it is celebrated for the successful preservation effort, the streamlined design that still looks fresh, and as a popular place for people to swim together next to the sea.

# 1936 MILLESGÅRDEN

### Carl Milles ▸ Stockholm, Sweden

The forest of pedestals on the Lower Terrace lifts Carl Milles's sculptures well above head height and makes reference to the smokestacks across Lake Värtan.

Art ran in the Milles family. Sculptor Carl Milles (1875–1955) is the most well known, with commissions spanning five decades in Sweden and the United States. His sister, Ruth Milles, was a sculptor, illustrator, and writer; the other woman in Carl's life, his wife, Olga, devoted herself to painting portraits; and Carl's half-brother, Evert Milles, was an architect. The Millesgården is the Milles family's most lasting creation, a synthesis of Carl's sculptures, Evert's buildings, and the landscape atop Herserud Cliff on the island of Lidingö in Stockholm.

The creation of Millesgården, which was guided primarily by Carl, began in 1906, when he and his wife bought cliff-top land and built their house atop it. The sculptor's success in the following decades allowed the property to grow southward down the slope, eventually comprising the house, a studio designed by Evert, a garden, and a series of terraces on different levels. Carl and Olga left for the United States in 1931—Carl worked most notably on the campus of Cranbrook Academy of Art outside Detroit (see *100 Years, 100 Buildings*), where he also taught—and they donated Millesgården to the Swedish people in 1936. The couple returned in 1950, when Carl created the large Lower Terrace modeled on Italian piazzas. Most recently and posthumously, an art gallery for temporary exhibitions was added to the property in 1999.

Just as many of Carl's sculptures were centerpieces of pools and fountains, such as *The Meeting of the Waters* in St. Louis, water is a theme connecting the various outdoor spaces for displaying his classically inspired bronze and stone sculptures at Millesgården. No less than five rectangular pools occupy the terraces to serve as settings for his "floating" sculptures, while figures spitting water turn the rocky hillside below the house and studio into an artificial water feature. Another theme is columns, which Carl salvaged from old buildings and integrated into the site as stand-alone elements. He also lifted the naked sculptural figures on columnar bases so people see them from below, silhouetted against the Stockholm sky. As a collection of his sculptures (many of them shipped over from the United States after the couple's return), Millesgården is exceptional, yet as an experience of art and landscape it is without compare.

# 1937 AMSTERDAMSE BOS

## Cornelis van Eesteren, Jacoba Mulder ▸ Amsterdam, Netherlands

In addition to the numerous recreational activities the park hosts, a network of trails for walking, bicycling, and horseback riding are found in the now dense forest.

At more than 2,400 acres (970 hectares), Amsterdamse Bos is the largest park in *100 Years, 100 Landscape Designs*, and probably the largest park created anywhere in the twentieth century. It is the equivalent of nearly three of New York's Central Park, and like that great nineteenth-century park, Amsterdamse Bos is a completely artificial creation that has grown to appear as if it has always existed.

As Amsterdam grew in the early decades of the twentieth century, biologist and activist J. P. Thijsse (see 1925) proposed a large landscape area of parkland at the eventual site of Amsterdamse Bos. Its realization came closer to reality when Amsterdam quadrupled itself through the annexation of neighboring councils, including the area proposed by Thijsse. In the early 1930s the Amsterdam Public Works Department began detailed plans for the park under architect Cornelis van Eesteren (1897–1988) and landscape architect Jacoba Mulder (1900–1988), with Thijsse as a consultant alongside a team of botanists, engineers, sociologists, and town planners. Inspired by German *Volksparks*, the duo approached the park's design and construction in terms that prioritized function over form, use over appearance. This truly modern approach pointed to the creation of a recreational park, with spaces for rowing, skiing (on a hill created from excavated fill), concerts, and camping—as well as a bird sanctuary and other ecologically minded elements—cut into large openings within a new forest of oaks and alder trees. One of the biggest tests came with how to plant a forest on polders (land reclaimed from the sea) that sat roughly 13 feet (4 meters) below sea level. The water level had to be lowered to allow sufficient room for tree roots, and species were selected based on their ability to absorb moisture and bind the earth.

Even though Amsterdamse Bos's scale pointed to modern construction methods, its realization, starting in 1934, coincided with the Great Depression, so the project served as a relief program for the unemployed and therefore was done with low-tech means. Nevertheless, the park was ceremoniously opened to the public by Queen Wilhelmina in 1937, though the forest that was planted the same year would not be "completed" for another thirty years. Now surrounded by dense urban development, Amsterdamse Bos is the most popular park in the Netherlands, annually serving 4.5 million visitors—nearly twice as many people as the whole Amsterdam metropolitan area.

# 1938 ALFRED CALDWELL LILY POOL

## Alfred Caldwell ▸ Chicago, Illinois, United States

A 2002 restoration led by landscape architect Ted Wolff involved, among other things, the removal and pruning of trees—many invasive—that were added in the decades after its 1938 completion.

Like his mentor Jens Jensen (see 1920), landscape architect Alfred Caldwell (1903–1998) approached his designs through a strong affinity for the native landscapes of Chicago and its surroundings. Although he would go on to realize some fairly large commissions with Ludwig Mies van der Rohe (notably the Illinois Institute of Technology campus and the grounds for the community of Lafayette Park in Detroit), his most intensely ideological landscape design came early in his career, with the renovation of a deteriorated Victorian-era lily pool in Lincoln Park.

At only 2.7 acres (1 hectare), the Alfred Caldwell Lily Pool—given the designer's name after a 2002 restoration—is a tiny part of the 1,214-acre (491-hectare) Lincoln Park, which stretches for more than 7 miles (11.2 kilometers) along Lake Michigan. It is easy to miss Caldwell's contribution to the park for more than just its size: sitting at the northeast corner of the popular Lincoln Park Zoo (at one point it served as the pool's rookery), the lily pool is tucked behind a thick line of trees on all sides. The main entrance is to the north, where a gate from the street is framed with limestone and timbers and hints at the joys this National Historic Landmark contains.

Once inside, a limestone pathway splits around the elongated pond that stretches across most of the site. The sound of water pulls visitors along the gently undulating path, whose stone surfaces bring them right up to the edge of the water. Caldwell added a "council ring," in the tradition of his mentor, but he also designed his own prairie-style statement: a timber and copper pavilion rooted to a stratified limestone base. This is the best spot to survey native trees, shrubs, and flowers in what Caldwell described as "a geological statement" and "a biographical footnote on the meaning of the Chicago Plain." In effect Caldwell crafted a miniature version of prehistoric glacial Lake Chicago, which drained southwestward about ten thousand years ago, exposing the limestone below. For Caldwell, nature was a mark of everything that came before, and his Lily Pool is a celebration of nature in Chicago—in the past, present, and future.

# 1939 TŌFUKU-JI TEMPLE HONDO GARDEN

**Mirei Shigemori** ▸ **Kyoto, Japan**

The photogenic north garden's random checkerboard pattern of square stones set on a field of moss foreshadows numerous contemporary gardens.

The jagged stones among the raked sand of the south garden are arranged in four groups that symbolize the Elysian islands: Eiju, Horai, Koryo, and Hojo.

One of the most historically stable types of garden design is *karesansui*, or dry landscape gardens, with many of the best examples found in the former capital of Japan, Kyoto. Created first in the fifteenth century as an aid to meditation, dry gardens evolved over time but stagnated and lacked innovation in modern times, at least according to Mirei Shigemori (1896–1975). The great designer and historian devoted himself to a contemporary renewal of dry gardens, and one of his strongest statements was his first major project, for the Tōfuku-ji Temple in southeast Kyoto.

Following studies of philosophy, art history, and the Japanese practices of the tea ceremony and ikebana (flower arranging), Shigemori moved from the countryside to Kyoto, where he was asked to write a book on gardens. He researched nearly one hundred of the gardens and traveled for three years in the 1930s documenting more than two-hundred-fifty gardens all over Japan, ultimately writing a twenty-six-volume encyclopedia on the subject. In 1938 he was contacted by the head priest of the Tōfuku-ji Temple, which dates back to 1239, to develop a one-hundred-year master plan for improvements to the Zen Buddhist complex. Seeing the area around the main building, the Hojo, as unsightly, Shigemori began by designing its Hondo Garden, which he called Hassô no Niwa—Garden of Eight Views—and completed in 1939.

The garden consists of four areas, one on each side of the rectangular hall. A clockwise path around the building brings visitors first to the southern garden with four stone settings in a dry garden and five moss-covered mounds in one corner. The western garden is made up of a checkerboard of recycled stone curbs, white sand, and shaped azaleas. The northern garden, made of square stones sitting in moss, is next, followed by the eastern garden, which features reused foundations from an old building arranged like the big dipper. The eight views, or mythical landscapes, correspond to the garden's major elements: four stone settings, moss mounds, checkerboard, moss field, and the Big Dipper. Although materials, such as the moss and the stones, recall traditional Japanese gardens, in Shigemori's hands even today they look different. This is nowhere more pronounced than in the north garden, where the designer applied points (stones) to a field (moss). Throughout this small garden, the balance of Zen simplicity and modern abstraction prevails.

# 1940 DUMBARTON OAKS

## Beatrix Farrand ▸ Washington, DC, United States

The Ellipse, with its central fountain, was designed by Beatrix Farrand with a perimeter wall of boxwoods, but the hedges' decline decades later led Alden Hopkins to replace them with a double row of clipped hornbeams.

Most landscape designs are notable simply because of what they are: the marks they make on the earth and the places they create for people. There are exceptions whose contributions extend into other realms of culture, such as the scientific information afforded by botanical gardens. Another instance is the Dumbarton Oaks Research Library and Collection; its Garden and Landscape Studies program is world-renowned and a fitting offshoot of the gardens that are considered the most complex and complete extant design by the great landscape gardener Beatrix Farrand (1872–1959).

Farrand was hired by Mildred Bliss in 1921 to design terraced gardens on the 53-acre (21-hectare) property she and her husband, diplomat Robert Woods Bliss, bought the year before as their country retreat. The former farm sat atop the highest point in the city's Georgetown neighborhood—it included a 100-foot (30-meter) drop from the house to the creek at the north end of the property—hence the need to terrace the gardens. Mildred collaborated with Farrand on the gardens for nearly thirty years, and they started with the Green Garden just north and east of the mansion and its new orangerie. Next to this garden for entertaining is the axial North Vista and down the hill are the Beech Terrace, designed around its enormous namesake tree; the Swimming Pool and Loggia that Farrand worked on with McKim, Mead & White; and the Ellipse, at a far remove from the house. Other terraced gardens were designed or reshaped by gardeners who followed in Farrand's footsteps, most notably the Pebble Garden with its intricate paving laid out by Ruth Havey with Mildred. Regardless, the gardens maintain Farrand's mix of formal and informal outdoor "rooms" that naturally follow the terrain.

In 1940 the land was broken up and parceled out, with the mansion and the upper 16 acres (6.5 hectares) given to Harvard University and the lower 37 acres (15 hectares) given over for a public park and the new Danish Embassy. One year later Farrand wrote *The Plant Book for Dumbarton Oaks*, which ensured the proper maintenance of the gardens and eventually their preservation. The book is seen as a precedent of sorts for the numerous books on garden and landscape studies that the institution continues to release, all the while giving scholars a beautiful setting for research on these topics.

# 1941 RED ROCKS PARK AND AMPHITHEATRE

**Burnham Hoyt** ▸ **Morrison, Colorado, United States**

Panoramic views from the Amphitheatre sitting between the 300-foot (91-meter) rock formations reportedly reach for 200 miles (322 kilometers).

Seeing a concert under the stars can be a memorable experience anywhere, but at Red Rocks Amphitheatre it is unforgettable. Sitting naturally between two massive rock formations, the venue is exceptional visually but also acoustically: Ship Rock (a.k.a. Titanic Rock) and Creation Rock, as they're called, provide echo-free acoustic perfection for any performance.

Red Rocks Amphitheatre has hosted a diverse range of musicians since it opened in June 1941, including the Beatles in 1964, but the dramatic site drew performers well before then. A number of concerts were held from 1906 to 1910 on a temporary platform set up by John Brisben Walker, who owned the land at the time and called it the "Gardens of the Titans." The City of Denver bought the land from Walker in 1928 and decided to turn it into a permanent open-air playhouse. The Depression-era Civilian Conservation Corps and Works Progress Administration (WPA) were called on to help realize the project, which was designed by Denver architect Burnham Hoyt (1887–1960). With so much determined by nature, there was little design for Hoyt to do. Seating made of wood, concrete, and stone curves between the rocks and stairs at the ends, while locally quarried red sandstone stacked into boxes serves as planters for evergreens. The trees cascade to the edge of the concrete-and-stone stage, which Hoyt modeled on the Dionysian Theater at the Athenian Acropolis. Steel framing, painted to match the rocks, supports a roof over the stage and hints at the tons of invisible steel that was required to anchor the new construction to the rocks.

Although the amphitheater that first opened to the public in 1941 is the draw, Red Rocks is also a 640-acre (259-hectare) park for hiking and biking, all located about 17 miles (27 kilometers) west of downtown Denver. Scattered with rock formations that, like the ones flanking the amphitheater, took sixty million years to create, the park is rife not only with scenic beauty, but also has a rich cultural history. Here Native Americans made camp, since this spot on the edge of the Rockies gave a panoramic view of any invaders approaching from the Plains to the east. Now concertgoers are the ones facing east, as they take in rock bands and other performances between the rocks. In 2015, one year before its seventy-fifth anniversary, Red Rocks Park and Amphitheatre was named a National Historic Landmark.

# 1942 GUSTAV-AMMANN-PARK

**Gustav Ammann** ▸ **Zürich, Switzerland**

Granite-flagged paths follow the pergolas across the park's high point (left) or descend to the pond adjacent to the building (right).

The pond, with its statue, was once a means of restoring harmony to factory workers during their leisure time.

Many of the great parks of the twenty-first century are built on the industrial remains of the past, such as a series of four parks (see 2002) in Zürich's Oerlikon district, which was home to factories but is now full of middle-class families and white-collar workers. These transformations bring to mind the lack of open space that must have existed when the factories were in full swing: where did workers go for rest from their long and grueling jobs? A World War II–era park in Oerlikon provides one answer.

Before the outbreak of the war, a number of European countries saw the creation of so-called welfare gardens, which gave factory workers a place to rest during their leisure time. Gustav Ammann (1885–1955), a founding member of the Association of Swiss Landscape Architects, was responsible for a welfare garden for the former machine tool factory Bührle & Co. in Oerlikon. Ammann, who worked with his son and frequent collaborator Peter Ammann on the job, was hired in 1939 to design a place of rest and recreation adjacent to a welfare house and canteen designed by architect Robert Winkler. The small site (less than an acre) benefited from southern exposure and a drop in elevation from the edges of the property down to the L-shaped building. In turn, the Ammanns placed overgrown pergolas along the perimeter ridge—to provide areas of solitude and create privacy from the adjacent buildings—and a more social area with a pond, statue, and tables and chairs adjacent to the building; simple lawns cover the slopes between the two domestically scaled areas. Completed in 1942, the pergolas and pond with stepping-stones express the influences of Japanese and Mediterranean gardens on Ammann's designs, though filtered through an alpine sensibility that valued natural stone and plantings.

In 1996 the garden was protected as a monument and then subsequently opened to the public and renamed Gustav-Ammann-Park in honor of the influential Swiss garden designer. In 2004 and 2005 the park underwent restoration work by Ryffel & Ryffel Landschaftsarchitekten, who restored the paving and stone walls, replaced many of the pergolas, and removed some of the trees and plantings. Regardless, to this day the park remains largely in its original state and a great example of a time when the welfare of workers found its antidote in nature.

# 1943 THE PARTERRE GARDEN

## Gudmund Nyeland Brandt, Poul Henningsen ▸ Copenhagen, Denmark

Although Poul Henningsen envisioned the small fountains to be made out of concrete, wartime conditions meant wood was used instead.

Not many cities can boast of a roller coaster sitting between their city hall and main train station. But Tivoli Gardens provides the Dæmonen roller coaster and numerous other rides, games, playgrounds, concerts, restaurants, and amusements on 40 acres (16 hectares) smack in the middle of Copenhagen. Yet as the name implies, gardens are at the heart of Tivoli. The Parterre Garden, in particular, adds some calm to the theme park while also marking its centennial.

Tivoli Gardens began fortuitously in 1843 when promoter Georg Carstensen managed to secure a five-year concession from the King of Denmark to erect an amusement park on land that was then just outside the city's West Gate. Carstensen laid out a summer garden with some permanent buildings, rides, and the signature lights that still enthrall visitors year-round. Although Tivoli has evolved in its nearly 175 years, a couple of things harken back to its origins: the zigzag layout of its paths, rows of trees, and lake that follow the city's old fortifications, and the king's dictate that permanent structures occupy no more than 25 percent of the property.

The Parterre Garden is a diminutive but important part of Tivoli's primarily open space, sitting at the northwestern end of its lake. Landscape architect G. N. Brandt (1878–1945) laid out the garden as a setting for perennial flowers, with paths winding between the parallel rows of planter beds. Within each are one or two shallow basins designed by Poul Henningsen (1894–1967), who served as head architect at Tivoli at the beginning of World War II. The designer's spiral lamps (similar to his famous PH Lamp) adorn the garden's edge, which is set off by a curving brick wall with benches that Henningsen was also responsible for.

This century the Parterre Garden was in considerably poor condition, so landscape architect Jane Schul (1943–) was hired to renovate the garden, which was carried out in 2006. New basins, paving, and plantings had to be installed, but all closely followed the originals. Even though many of the plantings could not be reused, Brandt's thorough documentation meant Schul could follow the spirit of the original garden, which provides visitors with respite amid the theme park's excitement.

# 1944 ELLSWORTH ROCK GARDENS

## Jack Ellsworth ▸ Kabetogama, Minnesota, United States

If any environment is embracing of so-called outsider art—creations made by self-taught individuals outside of traditional art academies and institutions—it is the outdoors, the realm beyond the four walls of a gallery. With some land, willpower, and vision, the landscape can become the canvas for any artistic statement. An enduring example is located where exposed rocks date back 2.8 billion years—older than those at the bottom of the Grand Canyon.

Voyageurs National Park spans 340 square miles (880 square kilometers) and, befitting Minnesota's "Land of 10,000 Lakes" nickname, features hundreds of islands spread across 130 square miles (337 square kilometers) of lakes. The Ellsworth Rock Gardens are located on the park's Kabetogama Peninsula, between two of the larger lakes: Kabetogama Lake, whose northern shore the gardens sit on, and Rainy Lake, which serves as the border between the United States and Canada. Needless to say, it is a remote property best reached by boat.

For about twenty years it was the summer home of Jack Ellsworth (1899–1974), a carpenter from Chicago, and his wife, Elsie. He built a cabin, outhouse, and workshop there in 1944, and between then and 1965 he shaped his masterpiece: sixty-two terraced flower beds with more than thirteen thousand lilies and a couple hundred sculptures made from local rock and concrete, all covering a 60-foot (18.3-meter) granite outcropping overlooking the lake. A dense forest served as a backdrop for the terraces that were connected by a system of meandering paths. The blooming annuals and perennials stood out against the trees, while the rock sculptures of animals, tables, altars, and other forms brought visitors to see "the showplace of Lake Kabetogama" in its heyday.

Yet from 1966, when he became ill, until his death in 1974 (Elsie died a few years later) Jack did not work on his gardens, so the forest took over the landscape, and the sculptures, buildings, and other structures deteriorated. The National Park Service acquired the property in 1978 as part of Voyageurs National Park, though it wasn't until 2000 that the park had enough funding to replace nonhistoric vegetation and repair buildings and sculptures. Since then an annual Garden Blitz maintains the Ellsworth Rock Gardens, but its current state merely hints at the original's synthesis of outsider art and flower-filled terraces.

Very little documentation of Jack Ellsworth's labor of love exists, so visitors must develop their own interpretations of the intuitive creation he is said to have devoted fourteen thousand hours of his life to.

# 1945 MARABOUPARKEN

## Hermelin & Wedborn ▸ Sundbyberg, Sweden

Marabou left Sundbyberg in 1976, but Nils Möllerberg's *Boxaren* (Boxer) and the other sculptures installed during Henning Throne-Holst's tenure illustrate the type of environment he created for his employees.

Although it sits in a bed of flowers, Arvid Knöppel's *Hjortdjur* (Deer) looks like it has cozied up to the pool for a drink of water.

When Sven Hermelin (1900–1984) started his business in 1926, he was the first person in Sweden to practice as a landscape consultant, rather than as a gardener contracted on design-build projects, as was the norm at the time. In 1941 he was joined by Inger Wedborn (1911–1969) and their partnership, Hermelin & Wedborn, lasted until 1968. Together they completed this park for the Marabou Chocolate Factory in Sundbyberg, just north of Stockholm. Today it serves as a public park and sculpture garden for the Marabouparken art gallery housed in the former factory.

Marabou was established in 1916 and started making chocolate three years later under director Henning Throne-Holst. In the 1930s the company was offered some land to grow, under the condition that the park for workers could be used by the public on weekends. Throne-Holst hired Hermelin to design the 5-acre (2-hectare) park in 1937, at which time he ventured to Britain to see how the Cadbury factory built a park for its employees. When it came to designing the park he looked to nature for inspiration, following from his contention that a designed landscape should look like it *grew* rather than was *planted*. Yet his assertion that "a lawn full of happy children is more beautiful than one full of colorful flower beds" clearly put people at the center of his designs. Hermelin carried out his initial work at Marabou until 1943, but with Wedborn he resumed work in 1945 and they maintained it together for another decade.

The landscape comprises two main areas that sit on either side of the site's 33-foot (10-meter) drop: a formal garden next to the former factory buildings up high, and an expansive lawn between trees that culminates in a swimming pool down low. With its pergola, fountains, hedges, and the art gallery and a restaurant in the old buildings today, the formal garden is the logical setting for most of the sculptures. A path through some trees descends to the lawn, whose narrow, tree-lined footprint leads toward the pool and pavilion, a popular, sunny spot at the western end of the site. Hermerlin & Wedborn treated the pool like a depression in the landscape, such that the grass extends all the way to the water. It's a subtle design detail, but one that perfectly illustrates how nature was the inspiration for creating a place people would enjoy.

# 1946 SAN ANTONIO RIVER WALK

## Robert H. H. Hugman ▸ San Antonio, Texas, United States

Since 1967 the steel-hulled, flat-bottomed barges have shuttled tourists along the River Walk, here paddling in front of the colorful umbrellas of Casa Rio.

The best pieces of urban infrastructure are those that don't appear to be infrastructure at all. Such is the case with the River Walk in downtown San Antonio. Lined with trees, walkways, shops, restaurants, hotels, and other amenities, it is San Antonio's leading tourist attraction—more popular than the Alamo. But it's also a part of a larger piece of infrastructure that was created last century to combat the floods that periodically ravaged downtown.

At the time of San Antonio de Valero, the late seventeenth-century mission settlement, the San Antonio River was a narrow, slow, meandering river that was as prone to drying up as it was to flooding. The gridded city subsequently grew in what was known as Bowen's Island, a peninsula formed by the southward-flowing river curving east, south, and then west—what would eventually be the River Walk. Every one-hundred-year flood would bring cries of flood control, but the dry spells between them lulled residents into a feeling of safety and the local politicians into inaction. Things changed after a 1921 flood, the worst in recorded history. Olmos Dam was completed upstream five years later and a new cutoff channel turned downtown from a peninsula into a literal island. Although a riverside park was completed in 1915 and some plantings along the banks of the river followed the cutoff's construction, no master plan existed for the river. In 1929 architect Robert Hugman (1902–1980) developed a plan with Spanish-style shops, restaurants, and outdoor cafés along the river. Construction started in 1939 and the Depression-era Works Progress Administration (WPA) handed over a twenty-one-block section of the River Walk to San Antonio two years later. The war derailed much from taking place along the river, but in 1946 Alfred Beyer opened Casa Rio Mexican Foods, the first café on the River Walk and a mainstay seven decades later.

Although Hugman lost his job on the River Walk in 1940, many of the stairs, bridges, walkways, and other features (including an outdoor theater with the stage and seating on opposite sides of the river) were built to his specifications. Subsequent designs, including an extension that linked downtown to the grounds of HemisFair '68, stayed within his "Old San Antonio" guidelines, resulting in a cohesive, timeless design that can be enjoyed while walking, eating, or riding a boat on the river.

# 1947 LUNUGANGA

## Geoffrey Bawa ▸ Bentota, Sri Lanka

In the lower garden, the Broad Walk extends into the distance at right, while the checkerboard rice fields alongside the lake are found at left.

The north terrace next to the house exhibits some gridded formality, but that gives way to informal spaces beyond the statues poised atop the retaining walls of the upper garden.

Geoffrey Bawa (1919–2003) is considered the greatest architect in Sri Lankan history. His most appealing buildings, such as the Kandalama Hotel (see *100 Years, 100 Buildings*) had a way of fusing with the landscape, appearing as if they grew out of or were completely encased by their surroundings. It's not surprising to learn then that Bawa's path away from law and toward architecture was prompted by a garden, the one he cultivated in Bentota for fifty years starting in 1947.

Lunuganga sits on 25 acres (10 hectares) of land jutting into Dedduwa Lake in southwestern Sri Lanka. Originally jungle, it was cleared and planted with cinnamon in the eighteenth century, and then cleared again and planted with rubber trees more recently. When Bawa bought it, the land was abandoned and uncared for, overgrown with vegetation that made it impossible to glimpse the lake from the existing house that he would expand over the decades. Bawa would also add smaller structures to the existing ones scattered about the site, but his first action was clearing: he removed rubber and hardwood trees to open up a vista from the hilltop house to the lake on the south. He called this area Cinnamon Hill, since it coincided with the plantation of cinnamon trees. The land was cleared of enveloping vegetation on other sides of the house to capture more views, and as this happened the contours of the land became more pronounced, "telling" Bawa how to proceed. This included the creation of terraces wrapping the house on the north, east, and west sides; the Field of Jars to the west, so named because of the immense, Ming-period Chinese jars scattered about; the Broad Walk running the length of the garden from east to west; and the adjacent rice fields that were cultivated three times a year.

Bawa considered the land around his house a garden within a larger garden, and not surprisingly his life here was spent predominantly outdoors. Now, visitors to the public gardens and the suites for rent on the lush, green Lunuganga estate can do the same.

# 1948 NÆRUM ALLOTMENT GARDENS

## Carl Theodor Sørensen ▸ Nærum, Denmark

The varied layouts of the individual gardens inside the oval hedges, as well as the spaces between the ovals, are apparent when seen from above.

Although allotment gardens, or community gardens for growing fruits and vegetables, are found in countries all over the world (see 1944), Denmark takes special pride in dating the phenomenon within its borders back to the mid-1600s, when small gardens were planted outside the fortress walls of Fredericia. The first modern allotment gardens in the country were created in 1821 near Aabenraa, gardens that are extant and protected by conservation laws. Also protected, but raising practical allotment gardens to the level of garden art, are the Nærum Allotment Gardens north of Copenhagen laid out by C. Th. Sørensen (1893–1979) in 1948.

Inspired by the courts of Renaissance and baroque buildings, as well as the writings of German landscape architect Leberecht Migge, who asserted that rolling terrain asks for curving lines while flat land prefers right angles, Sørensen used ovals to define the enclosures of forty allotments spread across the rolling lawn of a common green situated between public housing on one side and more traditional allotments on the other. (The ovals earned the project the Danish label *de runde haver*—the round gardens.) His initial plan, a regular grid of ovals spread across the site, gave way to a looser arrangement in which the ovals were laid across the curves of the slopes, resulting in a variety of vistas across the gardens and a dynamic flow through the interstitial spaces between the gardens.

Once Sørensen laid out the gardens, he prepared a seven-page booklet with guidelines and advice for the gardeners. Although each oval (technically an ellipse in geometric terms, laid out by two stakes and a long piece of string) was approximately 50 feet (15 meters) wide and 80 feet (24.3 meters) long—in the proportion of the Renaissance golden section—the individual gardeners were free to position their cottages, select the hedges, and lay out the interiors. In regard to the last, Sørensen provided four options to help the gardeners, but he stressed that his advice was a guide, not a directive. Even with such liberties embedded in the design, the gardens have some consistencies, particularly a preference for clipped over unclipped hedges, which make them a symbol of pride as well as history.

# 1949 SÍTIO ROBERTO BURLE MARX

**Roberto Burle Marx** ▸ **Rio de Janeiro, Brazil**

A wall composed of architectural fragments from Rio buildings serves as a background to the lily pool where old columns are capped with bromeliads.

Roberto Burle Marx (1909–1994) was the most influential, prolific, and original landscape architect in Brazil, much less in all of South America or arguably even the world. He created a distinctly Brazilian style of landscape that departed from any colonial precedents. Ironically, he discovered his approach to crafting indigenous gardens during a trip to Germany, the country of his father's birth, in 1928, when he happened upon some tropical plants in a botanical garden in Berlin—in search of his European roots, he found even deeper Brazilian roots.

In his long career in Brazil, Burle Marx was responsible for thousands of gardens, but his own garden in Rio de Janeiro's Barra de Guaratiba neighborhood, about 35 miles (56 kilometers) west of the downtown, is the most important, for it illustrates his broad artistic output, his ability to synthesize plantings and architectural elements into a remarkable whole, and his attempts at preserving Brazil's tropical plants. During Burle Marx's life-changing visit to Berlin, he was studying painting. The composition of his gardens—colorful plants and paving with flowing surfaces and lines—has often been attributed to his artistic training, as if he treated landscapes like paintings. Beyond that, his output was never limited to gardens; he continued to paint, but also created jewelry, sculpture, textiles, and glazed tiles. His gardens were the framework for this multifaceted output, and it is nowhere more pronounced than at the Sítio (a.k.a. Santo Antonio da Bica), since it served as a place of experimentation as well as his home. Here he could test out ideas for other projects, ideas rooted in the indigenous and tropical plants (more than thirty-five hundred species) that he collected on numerous expeditions throughout Brazil.

The 40-acre (16-hectare) former coffee plantation that Burle Marx purchased in 1949 was graced with remnants of rain forest as well as outcroppings of large boulders that he composed for aesthetic effect. He laid out the garden over four decades as a mix of formal and informal planting arrangements, the former predominantly by the house that frequent collaborator Lúcio Costa renovated. Alongside the tropical plants imported from the rain forest, Burle Marx added architectural fragments from old Rio buildings throughout the garden. These elements were used to construct a pavilion, the last piece added to the Sítio before Burle Marx donated the property in 1985 to the Brazilian government for posterity.

# 1950 PARQUE DA CIDADE ROBERTO BURLE MARX

**Roberto Burle Marx** ▸ **São José dos Campos, Brazil**

Parque da Cidade Roberto
Burle Marx sits on a
perfectly flat landscape
that is relieved by tall
Brazilian fern trees that
pull the eye upward.

The former residence of
Olivo Gomes, which is
propped up on columns
made from cast industrial
sewer pipes, juts out
over a pond added by
Roberto Burle Marx.

Although Roberto Burle Marx (1909–1994) was a prolific landscape architect with thousands of gardens to his name, he had a small cadre of architects whom he worked with on numerous occasions: Oscar Niemeyer, most notably at Pampulha (see *100 Years, 100 Buildings*) and the Brazilian capital of Brasilia; Lúcio Costa, who pushed Burle Marx into landscape architecture and restored his Sítio house (see 1949); and Rino Levi, who traveled with Burle Marx on his plant-hunting expedition into Brazil's rain forests and worked together on this project in São José dos Campos.

Most of Levi's commissions were situated in dense São Paulo, but the residence and textile mill for industrialist Olivo Gomes, located on 237 acres (96 hectares) 62 miles (100 kilometers) east of the metropolis, gave the architect the chance to build directly in nature. Working with architect Roberto de Cerqueira César, Levi designed an aggressively modern house that is lifted on round columns and projects toward the Burle Marx–designed landscape. Working without a plan, Burle Marx added a couple of lakes and an artificial island on the pancake-flat site, as well as a small pond bordered by azaleas in front of the house; a terrace jutting out over the pond became the signature feature of both the building and the landscape. The other side of the house—the approach side—features an *azulejo* (blue-and-white ceramic tile wall), a traditional technique that Burle Marx repopularized. The house and gardens were completed in 1950, though a second phase took place in 1965, with the addition of a children's garden, pool, and outdoor theater.

The residence and old textile mill were transformed into the Parque da Cidade Roberto Burle Marx in 1996. In addition to the gardens around the Olivo Gomes Residence, the municipal park features walking and bicycle trails, playgrounds, an environmental education center, a folklore museum, a pavilion for hosting cultural events, an outdoor theater, and a butterfly garden. More than a museum of a house and garden, the park is a thriving and important part of the community, born from the gardens of one of its most prominent residents.

# 1951 BROOKLYN HEIGHTS PROMENADE

## Clarke & Rapuano ▸ New York City, United States

A strip of trees, shrubs, and flowers sits in a fenced-in space between the walkway and private backyards.

Some of the most cherished public places arise from conflict. In New York's Brooklyn Heights neighborhood, that conflict came in the form of Robert Moses, the "power broker" who proposed barreling a six-lane highway through the heart of the community. Opposition by residents eventually led to the 1965 designation of the Brooklyn Heights neighborhood as the first landmark district in New York, and before that the creation of the Brooklyn Heights Promenade, a scenic walkway overlooking the East River and Lower Manhattan.

Between the two World Wars, Moses pushed through a number of projects that aimed at improving parts of "Old Brooklyn." These included surface transportation, such as new ramps for the Brooklyn and Manhattan Bridges, but also housing and the creation of the Borough's Civic Center. The Brooklyn-Queens Expressway (BQE), part of the postwar, citywide arterial highway program, was one of these projects, partially completed in the late 1940s. The stretch through Brooklyn Heights, with its nineteenth-century brownstones and row houses, was in the planning stage when a neighborhood association proposed an alternate scheme with stacked three-lane highways between a surface road at bottom and private gardens on top. Moses agreed to the plan, but changed the top surface to a public promenade beyond the backyards of the residents.

At just over a quarter-mile (half-kilometer), the esplanade is short, but it invites strolling and sitting to take in views of the southern tip of Manhattan. It overlooked the industrial piers jutting into the East River when it was completed in its entirety in 1951 (the southern section opened in 1950), but these views are now unencumbered thanks to the creation of the Brooklyn Bridge Park upon those piers; its first phase was completed in 2008. Unlike that park's varied design features catering to active city residents (and a huge berm that cuts down on the noise of the double-decker BQE), the design of the esplanade by Michael Rapuano (1904–1975) of landscape/engineering firm Clarke & Rapuano is simple and straightforward, with bluestone paving, iron railings, trees, and plenty of benches. Special moments occur at some of the six access points from the streets of Brooklyn Heights, particularly the circular terminus at the north end, where its complex paving patterns vie for attention with the skyline beyond.

# 1952 FUENTE DE TLÁLOC

## Diego Rivera ▸ Mexico City, Mexico

Since Diego Rivera depicted Tláloc on his back, his body rising only slightly above the water, the only way to obtain a decent view is a camera attached to a kite or, these days, a drone.

Diego Rivera's mural inside the Cárcamo de Dolores and the fountain in front are managed by Mexico City's Museo de Historia Natural.

Mexican artist Diego Rivera (1886–1957) was famous for two things: being married to Frida Kahlo and painting murals in his native country and in the United States. Yet in 1951 he received what he described in his autobiography as "the most fascinating commission of my career": a sculpture and fountain for the Lerma Water Supply System in Mexico City's huge Bosque de Chapultepec park.

Rivera was asked to paint his usual type of mural on four sides of a concrete tank inside the classical, rotunda-like Cárcamo de Dolores, a control station designed by Ricardo Rivas—typical except for the fact that the mural, called *Water, Origin of Life*, would be submerged underwater. In front of the building the artist worked in earth and stone mosaic rather than fresco to craft the large Fuente de Tláloc fountain—100 feet (30 meters) wide—which depicted the rain god Tláloc emerging from the slime, water spraying from his two-faced head into the basin. The murals depicted amoebas and other aquatic life positioned at the beginnings of evolution, though also the workers, architects, and engineers who built the city's extensive waterworks. The latter is a familiar theme from the artist who depicted industry in Detroit decades earlier, but the presence of the Atzec rain god outside was unexpected for Rivera. Nevertheless, Tláloc's presence is fitting, since at this spot in Mexico City the system tapped into the underground sources of the Lerma River and marked the ceremonial entry point for water entering the city's main reservoirs. Just as inside the artist celebrated the evolutionary role of water and the labor required to distribute it, outside he celebrated the cultural role of water in Mexican traditions.

From the completion of the fountain in 1952 and the murals a few years later, water was ever-present, meaning the murals deteriorated quickly, particularly those for which Rivera was unable to develop paints that would resist the water and the chemicals used to treat it. The whole was closed toward the end of the century and the water diverted into a pipe. An extensive restoration was completed in 2010, which reopened the artworks after they were closed to the public for more than a decade. Now Mexico City residents and tourists can see in one place two masterpieces celebrating the fusion of art and engineering—one long hidden and one a singular piece of earth art in a mythical guise.

# 1953 ABBY ALDRICH ROCKEFELLER SCULPTURE GARDEN

**Philip Johnson** ▸ **New York City, United States**

The museum's fifth-floor café provides the best overview of the sculpture garden and its balance of marble, water, plantings, and art.

Though less than an acre, the sculpture garden is suited for displaying monumental art, such as Barnett Newman's *Broken Obelisk*.

No visit to the Museum of Modern Art (MoMA) is complete without spending some time in the sculpture garden, whatever the season. Bound on three sides by MoMA's assemblage of buildings spanning sixty-five years and a tall fence on West 54th Street, the garden is an intimate, .5-acre (.2-hectare) space that is set up for looking at sculptures, taking in the occasional concert or special exhibition, or just sitting down to take a break from the museum's many galleries inside.

A garden for the display of sculptures has been part of the museum's program since 1939, when MoMA opened its International Style building on West 53rd Street designed by Philip L. Goodwin and Edward Durell Stone. Curators John McAndrew and Alfred Barr designed the sculpture garden basically as an outdoor gallery with curved and flat walls acting as backdrops for the art, but with very little landscape and only minor attempts to integrate it with the art and architecture. After Philip Johnson (1906–2005), who cocurated the museum's influential 1932 *Modern Architecture International Exhibition*, took the reins of the architecture and design department once again in 1946, he gained the commission to redesign the sculpture garden that would be named for the Rockefeller who secured the land for the original garden. Working with landscape architect James Fanning, Johnson created a space where art and landscape coexist in a pleasing and peaceful balance.

The size and extent of the sculpture garden that was dedicated in 1953 were modified during MoMA's expansions in 1964 (when Zion & Breen changed the plantings), 1984, and 2004, but the basics of Johnson's design are intact: two rectilinear pools, which he called canals, divide the marble-paved space into four "subrooms" that are further delineated by groups of trees and plantings. Offset from each other, the pools are bridged by marble slabs to connect the alternatively larger and smaller areas for the display of art. Depressed 2 feet (.6 meters), as if to turn the space into an outdoor "room," the garden is overlooked by the lobby on the west, a small café on the east, and the Modern restaurant on the south. But it's in one of the Bertoia chairs next to the pools where the garden's calming atmosphere can be best appreciated—even among the crowds of the highly successful museum.

# 1954 PEACE MEMORIAL PARK

## Kenzō Tange ▸ Hiroshima, Japan

Seen from the Hiroshima Peace Memorial Museum, the axis of water, sculptures, and trees culminates in the ruin of the A-Bomb Dome across the river.

The most destructive single event perpetrated by humans occurred on August 6, 1945, when the United States dropped an atomic bomb on Hiroshima and instantaneously destroyed a 4.6-square-mile (12-square-kilometer) area, killing about seventy-five thousand people instantly (and nearly twice that number all told when taking into account radiation fallout). Japan's surrender nine days later, following another bombing on Nagasaki, led to great uncertainty in the country as well as the need to rebuild. In turn, Hiroshima became a symbol for postwar reconstruction. With a positive view to the future following this destruction, it was decided that ground zero, once a thriving commercial center, would be turned into a place for peace.

The competition for Peace Memorial Park was held in 1949, won by a team led by architect Kenzō Tange (1913–2005). Since he attended high school in Hiroshima before university studies in Tokyo, Tange was attached to the city and had ideas for reconstruction even before the competition. His winning scheme defined an axis from an exhibition hall (now Hiroshima Peace Memorial Museum) raised on columns on the south to the so-called A-Bomb Dome on the north, whose remains somehow withstood the bomb blast centered overhead. In between was a large parabolic arch, reminiscent of Eero Saarinen's design for the Jefferson National Expansion Memorial in the United States (see 1968) and Le Corbusier's proposal for the Palace of the Soviets, a project that pushed Tange into architecture. North of the dome he envisioned sports and cultural facilities near the destroyed Hiroshima Castle (rebuilt in 1958), though his ambitious ideas that bridged architecture, landscape, and planning only found partial realization.

The Peace Memorial Park, which opened on April 1, 1954, sits on a peninsula in the delta of the Otagawa River. A path from the raised museum leads to an arched cenotaph designed by Tange after his attempt to have it created by Isamu Noguchi proved unsuccessful. Resembling an ancient Japanese house, the space under the arch frames the distant A-Bomb Dome, accentuating the survivor's importance in moving forward peacefully, in never repeating destruction on this scale again. In between is a linear pool that culminates in the Flame of Peace, which Tange added in 1964 and has burned continuously since. Trimmed shrubs and topiary trees soften the otherwise hardscape park, which was designated a place of scenic beauty in Japan in 2007.

# 1955 MELLON SQUARE

## Simonds and Simonds ▸ Pittsburgh, Pennsylvania, United States

Landscape architecture in the past one hundred years was not full of many firsts. Much of the groundbreaking work happened in previous centuries, but as cities grew—and grew taller—in the last century, the firsts concentrated there as open spaces were created in ever-more unique settings. Although San Francisco ripped up its Union Square to tuck a parking garage below it in 1942, Pittsburgh's Mellon Square can boast of being the first *modern* garden built over a parking garage.

Well before the plaza opened to the public in October 1955, the public space was badly needed. The "Golden Triangle," as the once industrial land between the Allegheny and Monongahela Rivers became known, had only one public space for 150 years. As "Steel City" transitioned to a downtown with banks and businesses beginning in the first half of the twentieth century, city leaders saw the soot that came with the steel as a barrier to luring new residents. So following World War II they embarked upon the three-decade-long "Pittsburgh Renaissance" to make the city more attractive for businesses and their employees, starting with the demolition of industrial buildings at the tip of the triangle of Point State Park. Tiny in comparison, Mellon Square was an integral part of the half-billion-dollar plan, since it provided a 1.3-acre (.5-hectare) block of green space in the middle of downtown.

Architecture firm Mitchell and Ritchey designed the six-level parking garage, while the eponymous landscape architecture firm of brothers John O. Simonds (1913–2005) and Philip O. Simonds (1916–1995) designed the plaza. John was the brother responsible for the design, and from the beginning he sketched a design with a central fountain. Over time he refined the plan and the details of the fountain's bronze basins, the surrounding planters, and the paving. The distinctive three-color terrazzo paving was a response to comments from Sarah Mellon, who wanted a pattern like St. Mark's in Venice, not rectangles. Triangles worked for John, since he had placed the entrances at the corners and this implied diagonal movement across the plaza.

Given this was the first building of a modern garden with trees and fountains above a parking garage, technical problems arose not long after completion. Combined with neglect and the plaza's ongoing popularity, Mellon Square underwent a pair of restorations, most recently in 2013, when some questionable flourishes from the 1987 restoration were undone, returning the plaza closer to its original state.

The slope of the site necessitated steps at Smithfield Street on the west, where a terraced fountain lures people up to the plaza.

Seen from William Penn Place on the east, Mellon Square is an island in the middle of downtown Pittsburgh that skillfully conceals the parking structure it sits above.

# 1956 VILLA SILVIO PELLICO

**Russell Page** ▸ **Moncalieri, Italy**

Russell Page (1906–1985) described himself as "the most famous garden designer no one has ever heard of." This self-effacing statement was far from accurate, given the number of gardens he produced, his royalty-studded client list, and the popularity of the single book he authored, *The Education of a Gardener*, from 1962. But the words are fitting when one considers how many of his gardens (mostly for private residences) were destroyed or maligned, a fate they might not have met if his fame was wider. A gem that has withstood the test of time is the garden he created at Villa Silvio Pellico in Moncalieri, just south of Turin.

The hilltop villa dates back to the eighteenth century and is named for the poet whose fame overshadowed that of his client, an owner of the estate in the 1800s. Signora Ajmone Marsan bought the estate in 1948 and in 1956 Page designed for her a neoclassical garden with modern touches. When he encountered the villa, it was just a lawn, a steep bank, and an unkempt kitchen garden. Marsan tasked Page to provide her with a viewing garden—a garden that would be most interesting when seen from the house.

So Page transformed the front of the house by laying out a series of six terraces on a south-facing axis: a vista with a square pool and geometric hedges in the foreground, the countryside in the distance, and a line of trees in between that served to block out the commune's buildings below. The steep bank was replaced with monumental stairs and stone walls that descend 20 feet (6 meters) from the lawn to the garden's outdoor "rooms." Instead of simply focusing on the main axis, Page created a shorter cross axis with a long pool on the left and a fountain on the right, both set perpendicular to the square pool. These spaces invite people to walk the terraces, which are defined by clipped hornbeams but also feature stone statuary that Page selected. The axial arrangement is classically Italian, but it is infused with modern touches, such as a subtle asymmetry and Page's use of plants in place of traditional Italian stonework.

Today, Villa Silvio Pellico is owned and carefully maintained by Emanuele Gamna and Raimonda Lanza di Trabia, who rent out two of the estate's buildings to vacationers and make the garden available for visits by appointment.

Although it looks like the gardens in this southern vista are flat, the terraces actually cover six levels as they descend from the lawn next to the house.

The pool in the foreground and the fountain beyond sit within well-defined "rooms" perpendicular to the main axis.

# 1957 PHILOPAPPOU HILL PATH

**Dimitris Pikionis** ▸ **Athens, Greece**

The Philopappou Hill Path culminates in an overlook with stone benches that invite people to take in the remarkable view of the Acropolis.

Dimitris Pikionis understood that when people walk they look at the ground more often than they look at what's around them.

If there is one ultimate site of intimidation for designing landscapes in the West, it is surely the Athenian Acropolis. For decades—centuries even—designers were not up to the task of providing suitable interventions around the Acropolis, which were needed to provide for the throngs of tourists visiting the ruins of the cradle of democracy. Yet Athens found the answer in one of its own, architect Dimitris Pikionis (1887–1968), who was born in the port city of Piraeus and who devoted nearly a decade to realizing his masterpiece in the shadow of history.

In the early 1930s Pikionis designed buildings in a distinctly modernist idiom, with flat, whitewashed walls and flat roofs, much like his contemporary Le Corbusier. But following the completion of some schools, one notably down the hill from the Acropolis, the architect broke with modernism in favor of reinterpretations of the Macedonian vernacular. This break coincided with an essay he wrote in 1935, "A Sentimental Topography," in which he "rejoiced in the progress of our body across the uneven surface of the earth" and found that "the same laws are at work in both nature and art." These lines foreshadow the work he would carry out at Philopappou Hill, but they also hint at the importance of walking in the architect's life. Elsewhere in the essay he railed against insensitive interventions within the Attic landscape. So in hindsight Pikionis was on a trajectory toward the paths overlooking the Acropolis.

When hired in 1951 by Konstantinos Karamanlis, the Minister of Public Works and future Prime Minister of Greece, to give some order to the Hill of the Muses and the Hill of the Nymphs, Pikionis started by clearing away past interventions, such as an asphalt road that connected the Odeon of Herodes Atticus with the Propylaea atop the Acropolis. With a project scope that was as much planning (of streets, alleys, intersections, and parking) as it was landscape design (of paving, retaining walls, parapets, pavilions, and the planting of cypress, pine, and olive trees), the resulting paths, completed in 1957, meld seamlessly with their surroundings. His success came from infusing then-current building methods with practices inspired by ancient arts, and through a devotion that led him to visit the site every day and direct masons in laying stones. The paths never repeat yet look like they have always been there—artistic lines at one with nature and his ancient predecessors.

# 1958 UNESCO GARDEN OF PEACE

**Isamu Noguchi** ▸ **Paris, France**

Beyond the benches and steles that Isamu Noguchi placed on the upper terrace is a concrete drum, the Meditation Space added by architect Tadao Ando in 1995.

The lower garden's complex composition of grass, stone, and water—seen here from the walkway—is barely visible below the mature trees.

Few twentieth-century artists embraced landscape as a medium as much as Isamu Noguchi (1904–1988), who was born in Los Angeles to an American mother and a Japanese father. From the garden he designed for Antonin Raymond's Reader's Digest Building in Tokyo in 1951 to the California Scenario sculpture garden in Orange County, Noguchi's trajectory moved toward larger works where space was a primary concern. The Garden of Peace he designed for UNESCO in Paris is an important part of Noguchi's oeuvre in this regard and a significant early example of an artist-created garden.

Noguchi received the commission in 1955 after architects Marcel Breuer, Pier Luigi Nervi, and Bernard Zehrfuss were selected to design the headquarters for UNESCO, which formed in November 1945. The artist was given a small area adjacent to one leg of the Y-shaped building. When an annex was made part of the building program, his commission grew to include a lower "Japanese garden" that would connect the main building and the annex. Noguchi's cross-cultural upbringing was just one indicator that his garden would recall Japanese precedents but that it would depart from them in more numerous ways. He traveled throughout Japan to select stones (some he would carve and some he would leave in their natural state), and he visited gardens and learned from master garden designer Mirei Shigemori (see 1939), but the resulting garden is more Noguchi than Japanese: he treated the earth like he treated stone—as a material to be carved.

The artist worked with Japanese gardener Toemon Sanô on the garden's construction from his return from Japan until its November 1958 completion. At the stone-paved upper patio, they installed concrete and stone seats and a large stone stele with an ideogram for "peace." From here the lower garden is visible in its entirety, unlike traditional Japanese gardens that are experienced fully through a stroll. A path of water follows the walkway leading to the annex and invites people to the lower garden, which is accessed by a trio of stepping-stones and an arched bridge at a right angle to the walkway. Granite pavers, grass mounds, and a pool that forms the ideogram for "heart" interlock to create a sculptural ground plane below the trees that Sanô selected to ensure some continuity with Japanese gardens. A major renovation and restoration completed in 2000 brought back the tranquilly expressive character of Noguchi's sculptural garden.

# 1959 LAS ARBOLEDAS

## Luis Barragán ▸ Mexico City, Mexico

The poetic means of integrating architectural elements (walls) with landscape elements (trees) is nowhere more striking than at the Bebedero fountain, seen here in two views.

The 1950s and 1960s were good years for Mexican architect Luis Barragán (1902–1988). In those decades he designed four residential subdivisions in the environs of Mexico City that shared one notably upper-class feature: horseback riding. Two of the four plans were realized, abutting each other on land about 14 miles (22.5 kilometers) from the center of Mexico City: Las Arboledas, which started construction in 1959, and Los Clubes, which followed about five years later.

For Las Arboledas, Barragán served as architect and client, the latter with investors who shared his passion for horses, something he had cultivated since growing up on a ranch. The streets were laid out on two large chunks of land bisected by the wide Paseo de Los Gigantes, and the plots were generously sized to accommodate houses and stables. He located the communal features according to the development's unique equine nature. Most famous among these are two fountains: Bebedero, located at the eastern end of the Paseo, and Campanario, situated farther west along the allée of eucalyptus trees that runs the length of the Paseo. Each fountain incorporates planar stucco walls and water, to define the otherwise open spaces between the lanes of traffic and to serve the horses. The long linear trough of Bebedero, which terminates in a tall white wall speckled with the shadows of the eucalyptus trees, is one of the most famous images in Barragán's oeuvre, and surely one that led to his 1980 Pritzker Architecture Prize. Although the community's horses have been replaced with dogs, it's easy to imagine the horses slurping at the trough and the riders resting in the shade.

Since Las Arboledas no longer serves its original purpose, the large house-and-stable lots have been cut up into smaller properties and a dense assemblage of red-tile-roof houses more typical of Mexico City's residential fabric. Those wishing to see one of Barragán's functioning designs for horses need to walk past Campanario to the west end of the Paseo, where a statue of the famous architect reclining on some steps is found, and head north to Los Clubes (a gated community) and the Cuadra San Cristóbal stables. The physical and thematic proximity of these two developments can be grasped in the fact Barragán designed a plan for a steeplechase tournament that spanned both. Fittingly, Bebedero and Campanario were way stations between the two places.

# 1960 STORM KING ART CENTER

## William Rutherford ▸ New Windsor, New York, United States

The land around Storm King is part of a state park whose many acres were donated by Ralph E. Ogden's company to preserve the hills as beautiful backdrops to the large-scale artworks, in this case Mark di Suvero's sculptures made from steel I beams.

Even though landscapes have long been a setting for artworks—going back at least to Roman Emperor Hadrian's second-century villa in Tivoli—the first modern sculpture park dates to around 1960 when two important ones were being created: the Kröller-Müller Museum (see 1961) in the Netherlands and the Storm King Art Center in New York's Hudson River valley. The latter, a U.S. counterpart to the European sculpture park, is notable for its dramatic setting but also its size, both of the grounds (now 500 acres [202 hectares]) and the artworks on display.

Ralph E. Ogden, who, along with H. Peter Stern, owned Star Expansion Company in Mountainville, New York, was inspired by the Kröller-Müller Museum's efforts to complete its sculpture park and donated 200 acres (81 hectares) in adjacent New Windsor for the creation of Storm King Art Center. The nonprofit institution opened to the public in 1960, using the Normandy-style château at its center to display local Hudson River School paintings—a commendable but not particularly ambitious start. That changed with Ogden's purchase of thirteen sculptures by David Smith in 1966, an act that pushed the landscape toward its current role as a setting for art. The Smith sculptures are grouped around the old building that now serves as Storm King's museum building; it hosts temporary, small-scale exhibitions and sits on the site's high point overlooking the rolling landscape extending to the north and south, where huge sculptures—most in steel—by Alexander Calder, Alexander Liberman, Mark di Suvero, and other familiar names make Smith's important works look domestic in size.

The man responsible for Storm King's landscape design was landscape architect William Rutherford (1917–2005), who worked on the site for twenty-five years. He dealt with grading, drainage, and other practical concerns, but his greatest task was to shape the landscape into a coherent whole. He also worked directly with artists to ensure that their sculptures found a synergy with the landscape. As Storm King grew over time to its present size, so did its landscape evolve: a gravel pit was filled, native-grass meadows were planted, a swamp was drained, formal gardens were removed, thick vegetation was thinned, and artworks were added. The whole is an informal landscape that invites wandering rather than a prescribed route. Its size ensures repeated visits are needed to take it all in.

# 1961 KRÖLLER-MÜLLER MUSEUM

## Jan Tijs Pieter Bijhouwer ▸ Otterlo, Netherlands

Marta Pan's *Floating sculpture, Otterlo* is visible at right in front of the low-slung museum that tries not to intrude on the landscape.

Artist Richard Serra sought out the bowl-shaped valley in the sculpture garden for *Spin out, for Robert Smithson*, which was installed in 1973.

A visit to the sculpture garden of the Kröller-Müller Museum in the center of the Netherlands is a visit to nature. The garden's more than 175 sculptures sit on 62 acres (25 hectares), but the museum and garden are found in the middle of the Hoge Veluwe National Park, which covers about 21 square miles (55 square kilometers). If the park is considered "the green heart of the Netherlands," then the sculpture garden is its soul.

The museum opened in 1938 when Helene Kröller-Müller, with her husband, Anton Kröller, realized a design by Henry van de Velde for displaying some of her nearly 11,500 artworks, mainly paintings, including a sizable collection of works by Vincent van Gogh. They owned the surrounding land that became the national park (it is still private and therefore requires an admission fee to enter) and donated their artworks and building to the Netherlands. In the early 1950s, the OKW (today's Ministry of Education, Culture, and Science) proposed a sculpture garden to sit east of the museum by a grove of trees. Museum director A. M. Hammacher hired landscape architect J. T. P. Bijhouwer (1898–1974) to lay out fifty to one hundred sculptures over the coming years, but delays meant that the sculpture garden only partially opened in 1961, with forty-three sculptures in place; a second phase followed soon after in 1965. Most unique about Bijhouwer's approach is that it was more of a strategic plan than a concrete design. Sculptures were placed informally within the meadows and forest, pulling people through the landscape with almost constant surprises. Renovations by Evert van Straaten in the 1970s (around the same time architect Wim Quist expanded the museum) and the firm West 8 this century followed Bijhouwer's path, so the experience of the sculpture garden is one of discovering art in a natural environment.

There are plenty of notable works among the many sculptures. Highlights include Marta Pan's *Floating sculpture, Otterlo*, specially commissioned for the 1961 opening, which literally floats in a pond close to the museum, and serves as an important transition between the museum and garden; Jean Dubuffet's playful *Jardin d'émail*; and Richard Serra's *Spin out, for Robert Smithson*, which sits in a clearing in the trees. Two pavilions, one by Aldo van Eyck and one by Gerrit Rietveld, were rebuilt on the sculpture garden, giving the museum space for small sculptures and adding architecture to the types of works on display.

# 1962 LAS POZAS

## Edward James ▸ Xilitla, Mexico

The Bamboo Palace is one of Edward James's most ambitious creations and situated in one of the most dramatic spots in Las Pozas.

Surrealism was a movement whose most well-known creations were paintings and sculptures—objects that could be displayed in museums. Surrealist environments—be they buildings or landscapes—were a rarity and Las Pozas in Mexico's state of San Luis Potosí is the best surviving example. While far removed geographically and culturally from England, the birthplace of Edward James (1907–1984), this is where he eventually found his psychological home in the jungle.

The son of an American railroad magnate and a Scottish aristocrat, James was set for life at the age of twenty-one, when he came into a huge inheritance. He was drawn to poetry, but to others his deep pockets made him more patron than artist; one artwork made for James was Salvador Dalí's famous *Lobster Telephone*. But with little outside appreciation of his poetry and a failed marriage, James left England for good at the start of World War II, first ending up in Los Angeles. There he heard about Xilitla, a town in Mexico's Huasteca region where orchids bloomed every November. He ventured there in 1947 and bought a former coffee plantation where he could grow the flowers. He did so each year until freezing temperatures killed eighteen thousand orchids overnight in 1962. Dejected, James reoriented his approach and vowed to cultivate things that could not be destroyed so easily, and so began the creation of his remote surrealist playground.

Two people were integral to James's realization of his jungle dream: Plutarco Gastelum first showed Xilitla to James and ended up living at Las Pozas, raising a family, and inheriting its 75 acres (30 hectares) after James died; José Aguilar Hernández turned James's sketches into a literally concrete reality. These drawings were made when James walked the property with his parrot and pig, and while this behavior could be chalked up to pure eccentricity, he truly wanted Las Pozas to be open—an environment for him, Gastelum's "substitute family," and alligators, monkeys, snakes, and other animals. The concrete structures built at Las Pozas—so named for the nine cascading pools formed by the river cutting through the site—mimicked natural forms and took on sometimes enigmatic names such as "The House with 3 Stories that Might Be 5." Open to the public since 1991, Las Pozas has been run by the Pedro and Elena Hernández Foundation since 2007.

# 1963 FONDAZIONE QUERINI STAMPALIA

## Carlo Scarpa ▸ Venice, Italy

The linear fountain ending in a circular receptacle gives the small garden a definite sense of direction and movement.

The square basin at one end of the garden was salvaged from Carlo Scarpa's design for the Veneto pavilion at Expo 61 in Turin.

The few modern interventions that do exist in Venice hide behind the historic cityscape's Gothic facades. One of the best examples that incorporates both a modern interior and landscape, *and* is open to the public, is found at the Fondazione Querini Stampalia, which native son Carlo Scarpa (1906–1978) renovated starting in 1949. The small garden at the rear of the sixteenth-century palazzo exhibits Scarpa's penchant for details, which work together to subtly reference its watery Venetian context.

The Fondazione Querini Stampalia dates back to 1869, when Count Giovanni Querini, the last descendant of the Querini Stampalia family, created it for study purposes. Shortly after Giuseppe Mazzariol took over as the foundation's president in 1957, he hired Scarpa to restore and renovate the interiors, the garden, and a new footbridge leading to the entrance. Even before visitors set foot on the bridge, they could see through the entrance gates, water room, and ground-floor exhibition space all the way to the green grass of the garden beyond (the same effect remains to this day, although a new bridge has deemed the Scarpa original mere eye candy). A joint design of sorts, with Mazzariol selecting the plantings that would go into Scarpa's design, the garden, alongside the interior renovations, was completed in 1963.

The rectangular garden is accessed through glass doors at the back of the ground-floor gallery, where the stone and concrete floor extends from inside to outside. The lawn seen from a distance sits in front, behind a low concrete wall at about waist-height. A channel with water flowing left to right splashes into a sculptural stone basin, the sound enticing people to follow the water to the other end of the garden. There a mazelike sculpture carved from alabaster is found to be the source of the fountain, while beyond it is a square pond in the middle of a large bronze tray. Behind the pond is a rough concrete wall with a horizontal line inscribed with mosaics from nearby Murano. An alternate route around the garden passes over the lawn on stepping-stones, which make the raised plane resemble a surface of water rather than grass. Although concrete, grass, and stone are the predominant surfaces throughout, the garden's design is all about water, as something to be seen, heard, and touched, but also as a metaphor for Venice's precarious existence.

# 1964 JOHN DEERE WORLD HEADQUARTERS

## Sasaki Associates ▸ Moline, Illinois, United States

Henry Moore's *Hill Arches* sits on an accessible island in the middle of the Upper Lake adjacent to the office building.

It's more than fitting that the corporate headquarters of John Deere, one of the most popular brands of riding lawn mowers, would be covered in a landscape of well-manicured lawns. Today, more than 140 acres (57 hectares) of the company's 1,200-acre (486-hectare) campus are mowed. At just over ten percent, this may not seem like much, but it is much more than what was originally envisioned in the landscape design by the firm of Hideo Sasaki (1919–2000).

Everything changed in 1963 when Deere & Company—focused on farm implements and machinery since John Deere developed the self-scouring steel plow in 1837—entered the consumer market with lawn mowers, lawn tractors, and snowblowers. Thereafter the grounds became a billboard for what their products were capable of, which was prescient considering that three hundred thousand people in one year flocked to the campus after Deere & Company moved from downtown Moline to its outskirts in 1964. Those visitors, like the ones who still make the trek to the city on the Iowa border, went to see the administration building and the exhibition hall designed by Eero Saarinen as much as Deere's line of products. Saarinen, who died unexpectedly in 1961 and therefore never saw his project completed (colleagues Kevin Roche and John Dinkeloo finished the project and added a second wing to the central building), designed the buildings to be clad entirely in glass and COR-TEN steel, whose weathered surfaces harmonize with the wooded landscape.

Saarinen hired Sasaki to develop the site plan and the grounds, which consisted of thousands of elms and a natural ravine that sloped toward the road (now John Deere Parkway) and the farm fields beyond. Saarinen placed the eight-story administrative building in the hollow of the ravine, so it acted like a dam next to the two lakes stretching out in front of it—one ornamental and one for storm water and heat exchange for the air-conditioning systems. The three buildings, with their exposed COR-TEN steel structure and louvers, are unabashedly aggressive marks in Sasaki's pastoral landscape, which had to include thousands of new trees to replace those lost to Dutch elm disease. As initially designed, flowering plants would have grown beneath the new and old trees, turning the site into a Midwestern woodland. But then the lawn mowers came and so did the acres of lawn. It is mechanized reality where Saarinen's buildings are mechanical aesthetics.

# 1965 THE SEA RANCH

## Lawrence Halprin ▸ Sonoma County, California, United States

The shed roof of Charles Moore's Condominium One follows the windswept line of the hedgerow, as if both building and landscape were shaped by nature.

At 5,000 acres (2,000 hectares), the Sea Ranch community in Northern California is, by leaps and bounds, the largest project in this book. At this size, design is less about plant selection and the creation of gardens, and more about large-scale marks on the land, the preservation of natural features, and the definition of guidelines for residents to follow as the community evolves. That the half-century-old development has retained the qualities that predated the development and has been a continuously popular place for living and vacationing means Lawrence Halprin (1916–2009) did something right when he first sketched out his ideas for the coastal site.

In 1963 Oceanic Properties, the California arm of Hawaii's Castle & Cooke, bought ten miles of rugged coastal land in Sonoma County that previously served as the Del Mar Ranch. Halprin was hired to develop the landscape and master plan for the site that extended about one mile inland and straddled Highway One. Well before sheep and cattle grazed the many acres, the Pomo Indians made seasonal trips to the coast to fish, a history Halprin would tap into with the "living lightly on the land" ethos he would apply. Maintaining the essential character of the landscape was paramount, and its stewardship would be ensured by the 111-page declaration of covenants that was delivered to Sonoma County on May 10, 1965, establishing the Sea Ranch.

Halprin's approach, which looked back deeply in time and forward across future generations, privileged nature over buildings, though fortunately the prototypical residences (by Charles Moore, Joseph Esherick, and others) took on forms and materials that integrated with the site in a manner that is now unmistakably Sea Ranch. The rich coastal landscape of beaches and cliffs would be shared, with access provided by trails (some made public). Behind the coastline houses clustered next to cypress hedgerows for protection from strong Pacific winds. Native plants and trees were privileged over all else, to make sure the landscaping would thrive in the harsh conditions and host wildlife that would coexist with the residents; these numbered around nine hundred as of the fiftieth anniversary of the Sea Ranch's incorporation. Although the ocean views and evolving natural beauty of the place remain the privilege of a select few, rentals and rooms at the Sea Ranch Lodge allow others the chance to "live lightly on the land" for at least a few days.

# 1966 PISCINA DAS MARÉS

## Álvaro Siza ▸ Leça da Palmeira, Portugal

When full, the water in the main pool covers part of the rocks to confuse distinctions between built and existing, man-made and natural.

Drivers zooming along the Atlantic coast on Avenida da Liberdade north of Porto would be forgiven for missing the Piscina das Marés (Pool of the Sea); the two outdoor pools with changing facilities are set nearly 10 feet (3 meters) below the roadway. The hidden nature of the project also arises from the approach of Porto-based architect Álvaro Siza (1933–), who strove to merge the built structures with the rocky landscape.

The seaside pool was not the first municipal pool that Siza realized in the parish of Leça da Palmeira, nor his first project along the coast; the earlier Boa Nova Tea House is a fifteen-minute walk north. One year before it opened in 1966 he completed a pool in Quinta da Conceição Park. Although the settings—a rocky coast and a tree-lined park—are diametrically opposed, Siza designed each pool similarly, using the changing facilities as an architectural promenade that concealed and then revealed the landscape. Of these two, the Piscina das Marés is more dramatic and more beloved: it was named a local landmark on its fortieth anniversary in 2006.

After parking in the lot next to Avenida da Liberdade, bathers catch a glimpse of the two saltwater pools set carefully into the rocks below. As they descend the ramp between parallel concrete walls toward the changing rooms, the vista disappears and all that remains is sky. Bathers follow more concrete parallel walls before encountering V-shaped walls outside that redirect them toward the pools. In this promenade the changing rooms act as a transition between the controlled, man-made realm of the city and the rough, natural coast of rock, sand, and water.

In his writings, Siza explained that the natural conditions had "already started to design the swimming pool." So after surveying the land he placed two concrete walls perpendicular to the coast and huge rocks to form the main pool. The smaller children's pool is set back, tucked between more rocks, bound on one side by a curving concrete wall, and accessed by a child-size passage under a concrete walkway. The simple palette of concrete walls, walkways, and stairs allowed Siza to create subtle transitions between the rocks and to fit the pools so blasting wasn't necessary, important given the low budget. Yet lack of money did not mean lack of inspiration: the pool is a lasting integration of architecture and landscape.

# 1967 PALEY PARK

### Zion & Breen ▸ New York City, United States

The water, the Eero Saarinen
tables and Harry Bertoia
chairs, and a canopy of
seventeen locust trees
invite people to stay a while.

The notion that a small space can have a large impact is seen most dramatically in this pocket park designed by Robert Zion (1921–2000) of the landscape firm Zion & Breen with architect Albert Preston Moore. Occupying a lot only 42 feet (12.8 meters) wide and 100 feet (30.4 meters) deep, what Paley Park lacks in size it makes up for in the simple yet dramatic articulation of water, plantings, and tables and chairs. Designed as the first of a hoped-for hundred throughout the city, unfortunately very few were ever built, leaving Paley Park as just a taste of what could have been.

Many of the parks and plazas that *did* follow Paley Park are what New York defines as privately owned public spaces, where developers could add extra floors to their buildings in exchange for providing a public amenity. But Paley Park is unique in that it's entirely private (but open to the public). William S. Paley, then chairman of the board of CBS, created the park in honor of his father, Samuel, who died in 1963. A few years after Zion outlined his vision for the many small parks that would be located where people work and shop, Paley worked with him on transforming the site of the former Stork Club into the original vest pocket park. Zion envisioned one vest pocket park for each Midtown Manhattan block, a series of outdoor "rooms" human in scale with walls, floors, ceilings (tree canopies), seating, waterworks, plants, and kiosks.

Although common to New Yorkers who work or shop in the area, Paley Park comes as a surprise to a lot of people who encounter it. As observed by William H. Whyte about a decade after its 1967 completion, many passersby would do a double take when walking along East 53rd Street, then turn and ascend the four steps into the park. Its already narrow width pinched by a small kiosk and maintenance closet, the park opens up past the steps toward the main draw: the rear waterfall. Recirculating 1,800 gallons (6,800 liters) per minute, the wall of water effectively drowns out the traffic and other sounds of the city. The rest of the space is a grid of locust trees, granite paving, movable tables and chairs (rare at the time), vines climbing the side brick walls, and continuous stone benches in front of the walls—most of which was carefully replaced in a 1999 renovation. It is a simple concept that should have been highly replicable.

# 1968 JEFFERSON NATIONAL EXPANSION MEMORIAL

## Eero Saarinen, Dan Kiley ▸ St. Louis, Missouri, United States

Early opponents of Eero Saarinen's design pointed out its similarity to an unbuilt, Fascist-era proposal for Rome, which faded into time as the Gateway Arch—reflected in one of Dan Kiley's pools—became one of the most recognizable monuments in the world.

The symbols of cities often veer to buildings and skylines (think of the Eiffel Tower and the Manhattan skyline). More rarely does a memorial or landscape take on that role. Most successful in this regard is the Gateway Arch, the symbol of St. Louis, the most notable component of the more expansive Jefferson National Expansion Memorial, and one of the most famous memorials ever created.

The memorial was officially dedicated on May 25, 1968, two decades after a team led by architect Eero Saarinen (1910–1961) won the 1947–48 architectural competition. A dozen years before that, city leaders approached the federal government with the idea of razing a forty-block section of downtown and turning it into a riverfront park memorializing the Louisiana Purchase. By the time the competition was held, St. Louis's plans were well known and the city received 172 submissions. Some people pegged Eliel Saarinen, Eero's father, to win, but Eero's 630-foot (192-meter) catenary arch rising from a wooded landscape designed by landscape architect Dan Kiley (1912–2004) was victorious in the end, described by the jury as "an abstract form peculiarly happy in its symbolism."

Although the 91-acre (37-hectare) site—the largest cast iron district outside of New York's SoHo—was cleared by the start of World War II, construction of the memorial did not commence until February 1961. Saarinen was able to develop the details of the Arch until his untimely death in 1961, and Kiley worked on the landscape until 1964, when landscape architects staffed by the National Park Service (NPS) took over. Kiley's final design placed curvilinear ponds near the Arch legs, groves of trees by the lawns, and nine hundred poplars in allées along wide walkways. NPS made significant changes to his design, such as changing the poplars to ashes, when the service finally realized the plan in the 1970s.

More changes to Kiley's landscape came in 2009 when a team led by landscape architect Michael Van Valkenburgh won a competition to better connect the Arch grounds to downtown St. Louis on the west and the Mississippi River on the east: a series of ramps would make the riverfront fully accessible, while also serving as a flood control barrier; and a landscape bridge over Interstate 44 would improve access to the Arch and the expanded below-grade museum beneath it. Work on the CityArchRiver project was scheduled to be completed in summer 2017.

# 1969 OAKLAND MUSEUM OF CALIFORNIA

## Dan Kiley ▸ Oakland, California, United States

Although Dan Kiley strove to soften the rigid geometry of the concrete structure through the "lacy veil" of Japanese pear trees, the clipped shrubs reinforce the lines of the terraced rooftop.

It is not uncommon for designers to strive to merge buildings and landscape, but it is a feat that is rarely pulled off well. The Oakland Museum of California is a magnificent exception, a terraced mass of concrete that is softened by abundant plantings that cover its roof.

The competition for what began as simply the Oakland Museum took place in September 1961, the month of architect Eero Saarinen's untimely death. The client, made up of Oakland citizens who wanted to build three museums—of art, culture, and natural science—on a large, four-block site near Lake Merritt, invited Saarinen's successors, Kevin Roche and John Dinkeloo, out of respect. They won the competition with a scheme that combined the three institutions into one building: stacked, terraced, and covered with a park, the last in reference to nineteenth-century plans that revealed the site was intended to be a park before it was taken over by commercial development. For lead designer Roche, the landscaped terraces would function as extensions of the interior galleries, playing a part in explaining the art, culture, and nature of California.

The architects brought on landscape architect Dan Kiley (1912–2004), who had worked with Saarinen on the Miller House and Garden and with Roche on the Ford Foundation (see *100 Years, 100 Buildings* for both), and he in turn worked with California horticultural consultant Geraldine Knight Scott. By the time Kiley came on board, Roche's design was basically complete, with an armature of concrete steps, balconies, shelves, and planting troughs ready to be filled with trees, shrubs, vines, and other living material. Kiley described the task as equal parts engineering and curating: selecting plantings that would not overload the roof structure but would survive in the shallow beds and meaningfully portray the state's flora. Species were grouped according to soil, light, and moisture requirements, and included climbing vines, creeping ground cover, dense shrubs, and small trees. The 7-acre (2.8-hectare) terraces and adjacent garden were completed in 1969, and a renovation and expansion project wrapped up in 2013. The latter focused on the building entrances and interior galleries, so the rooftop landscape that merges with the building is basically the same as it was more than forty years ago.

# 1970 SPIRAL JETTY

### Robert Smithson ▸ Rozel Point, Utah, United States

This aerial view of *Spiral Jetty*, located on the northeast shore of the Great Salt Lake, was taken when the waters were high and had the cloudy red color that Robert Smithson appreciated.

Land art was a movement that arose from two very American conditions: the open spaces of the West and New York's gallery scene. New York's arts patronage, most notably gallerist Virginia Dwan, enabled artists Robert Smithson (1938–1973), his wife, Nancy Holt, Michael Heizer, and Walter De Maria to construct permanent artworks in the 1970s in Utah, Nevada, and New Mexico—far away from the city's galleries. Smithson's *Spiral Jetty* is one of the earliest and most significant examples of artists breaking outside of the gallery's confines to confront the natural landscape.

After the Land art baby steps of documenting industrial monuments in his photographic essay "The Monuments of Passaic" and crafting sculptures out of dirt and mirrors, Smithson launched into finding a location that would become his famous *Spiral Jetty*. Intrigued by a phenomenon he heard about in which lake water turned red from certain microbes, the artist found such a spot on the northern end of the Great Salt Lake in Utah. Further inspired by the spiral structure of salt crystals and a legend that the lake was connected to the ocean via an underground channel that would reveal itself as a whirlpool, Smithson envisioned an artwork that would capture "a spinning sensation without movement."

In April 1970, after finding a contractor daring enough to work with him, Smithson started work on building *Spiral Jetty*, a counterclockwise spiral measuring 1,500 feet (457 meters) long, 15 feet (4.5 meters) wide made from 6,650 tons of basalt rock. Amazingly, it took only three weeks to complete. Smithson walked in and out of the lake to stake out the path of the spiral, and the contractor, Bob Phillips, and his crew followed with truckload after truckload of rock stacked to Smithson's specifications. Phillips asserted that the rocks had to be mounded like a dike, but the artist didn't budge in his demand for a relatively flat surface with the rocks slightly higher along the edges. This profile means people who go to the effort to find *Spiral Jetty* can traverse it to its center, but it also means that the artwork was submerged for most of its nearly fifty-year existence. In 2002, three years after Smithson's estate donated the artwork to the Dia Art Foundation, the salt-encrusted jetty reappeared, enticing another generation of fans of Land art to the shores of the Great Salt Lake and revealing the environmental predicament that has seen the lake depleted to near-record levels.

# 1971 TUCSON CONVENTION CENTER

**Garrett Eckbo** ▸ **Tucson, Arizona, United States**

The large boulders that pepper the public spaces, here seen in the Fountain Plaza, were reportedly taken from Sabino Canyon in the nearby Santa Catalina Mountains.

Statistically 1970 was the first time the U.S. Census recorded more people living in suburbs than cities. Confronted with dwindling populations, American cities in the late 1960s and early 1970s undertook urban renewal projects to lure people back downtown. This is when Tucson embarked on its own attempt at urban renewal, creating the three-building Tucson Community Center (TCC) and knitting it together with a network of public spaces.

Local architecture firms Cain, Nelson & Wares and Friedman & Jobusch were responsible for the buildings: the Tucson Arena, the Leo Rich Theater, and the Tucson Music Hall. For the 5.75-acre (2.3-hectare) public space, the City of Tucson called on the large and prominent San Francisco landscape architecture firm Eckbo, Dean, Austin and Williams (later EDAW). As in many of the firm's projects, Garrett Eckbo (1910–2000) was the lead designer for the TCC, which was ideal for Tucson since Eckbo saw landscape design as a social art. He wanted the public spaces in Tucson to bring back the people displaced by the urban renewal, while also inviting new expressions of ideas. The buildings and landscapes opened in two stages between 1971 and 1973, but by the 1980s the "Community" in TCC was dropped in favor of "Convention," shifting the social ideas toward commercial and tourist concerns. The public spaces Eckbo designed fell into disrepair in the ensuing decades, but a recent push by preservationists—and the project being added to the National Register of Historic Places in 2015—has moved things in a more positive direction.

The TCC landscape consists of four distinct elements: the Fountain Plaza, the Upper Plaza, Veinte de Agosto Park, and the Walkway. The first three were completed in 1971 and the last came in 1973, linking them into an ensemble. Fountain Plaza, taking up nearly half of the acreage, is the most dramatic, with groves of African sumac trees, cascading water features, and large boulders. The Upper Plaza has more native trees, though its original fountain was replaced by a large sculpture. Veinte de Agosto Park, with its mature trees making it a popular lunch spot, sits on a triangular island north of the others. Lastly, the narrow Walkway is marked by a water channel and a series of sculptural obelisks. The water, native plantings, and boulders throughout show that Eckbo was in tune with the desert landscape and adept at crafting spaces everybody could use.

# 1972 OLYMPIAPARK MÜNCHEN

## Behnisch & Partner, Günther Grzimek ▸ Munich, Germany

Construction began in 1965 on a TV tower measuring 954 feet (291 meters) tall, seen here from atop "rubble mountain," one year before Munich even considered hosting the Olympics.

As seen from the top of the TV tower, the ground continues beneath the roofs of the three stadiums in an expression of democracy— freedom of movement.

In 1966, thirty years after the Olympics were held in Berlin under the Nazi regime, Munich won the bid to host the 1972 Summer Olympics, the Games of the XX Olympiad. The opportunity enabled a democratic West German government to break from its National Socialist past and project to an international audience the country's tolerance and liberalism, in part through the expression of buildings and landscapes. Although the sporting events were overshadowed by the massacre of Israeli hostages, Olympiapark München has remained a lasting symbol of the country's political aspirations and a popular recreation spot.

Upon winning the bid, the Olympic organizers in Munich selected designer Otl Aicher to lead the design department for the Games. In addition to designing the famous pictograms and the Olympic mascot—the dachshund Waldi—Aicher helped set the tone for the Games, which was in opposition to the 1936 Games: celebratory and playful instead of monumental and military. In 1967 Stuttgart's Behnisch & Partner, led by Günter Behnisch (1922–2010), won a competition to design the stadiums and landscape with a scheme that consisted of tentlike roofs over the undulating Oberwiesenfeld landscape, a large brownfield site of close to 700 acres (280 hectares) north of the city. That same year engineer Frei Otto created a tensile canopy structure for the German pavilion at Expo 67 in Montreal; his design influenced Behnisch & Partners' competition-winning design and eventually he was brought on to help realize the stadiums' glass roofs.

Although the three photogenic stadiums remain the most important architectonic contributions of the 1972 Olympic Games, the landscape design is a vital component. It was overseen by Günther Grzimek (1915–1996), one of the few progressive landscape designers in Germany in the 1960s. Confronted with an uneven site marked by "rubble mountain," a peak formed by debris from WWII bombing raids, construction involved the moving of more than two million cubic meters of earth and the planting of thousands of trees, shrubs, and plants. A small stream cutting across the site was dammed to create a lake at its heart—stadiums to the north, and rubble mountain (made taller from stadium construction), undulating lawns, and clumps of oak and pine trees to the south. The stadiums remain popular venues for concerts, festivals, and sporting events, just as the landscape is a draw for walks, picnics, wintertime sledding, and other types of recreation.

# 1973 JARDIN ZEN

## Erik Borja ▸ Beaumont-Monteux, France

Of all the culturally and geographically specific types of gardens, the Japanese Zen garden is the most lasting, popular, and exportable. A simple palette of moss, rocks, and water as a meditative microcosm of nature dates back to fifteenth-century Kyoto but is found now in every corner of the globe, on plots of land large and small, and even in tiny toy containers that can be taken anywhere. The gardens are easy to appreciate but require intense learning, practice, and patience to understand and perfect. One of the most impressive examples outside Japan is found in the Drôme area in southeastern France.

Artist-turned-gardener Erik Borja (1941–) began working on the gardens around his summer residence in Beaumont-Monteux in 1973, when he lived and worked in Paris. Four years later he embarked on a trip to Japan to study the gardens of Zen Buddhist monasteries in Kyoto and Nara (the capital before Kyoto). The gardens he visited made such an impression that by 1979 he had moved his Parisian workshop to Drôme and reoriented the designs of the gardens based on what he had learned. Instead of merely applying the aesthetics of the Japanese gardens to his property, Borja strove to apply the deeper principles of Zen gardens to the French landscape, resulting in an East-West synthesis.

Borja would lay out five gardens east of the house, where the undulating land slopes down to a river on the eastern edge of the property. First was the small Meditation Garden cradled by the L-shaped house, though in time it grew to encompass a "pool" covered with white gravel and a real pool filled with water. The Tea Garden stretches out to the east, using the Mediterranean Garden as a backdrop. Borja made a departure from these overtly Japanese gardens with what he called the "cultivated paradoxes" of the next three gardens: the terraced Mediterranean Garden made from salvaged stones to resemble a ruin; the Southern Garden oriented around pools created next to three two-hundred-year-old oak trees; and the River Garden, which taught him that nature had to be understood, not controlled, when the river flooded and destroyed the work. On a relatively small 7.5 acres (3 hectares), the self-taught Borja was able to craft a handful of distinct, sculptural gardens that are remarkable for their variety, cohesion, and thorough attention to detail.

# 1974 FORT WORTH WATER GARDENS

## Johnson/Burgee ▸ Fort Worth, Texas, United States

Water rushes into the Active Pool, where Johnson and Burgee provided precarious steps for people to descend to the pentagonal basin.

The Dancing Pool (a.k.a. the Aerating Pool) is surrounded by plenty of tiered seats for people to watch the mesmerizing display of water droplets dancing in the air.

At one point in his long career, New York architect Philip Johnson (1906–2005) asserted that his best work was in Texas. Most likely he was referring to a few of his buildings—Republic Bank Center and Pennzoil Place in Houston, and the Amon Carter Museum of American Art in Fort Worth—but also to the Fort Worth Water Gardens, a 4-acre (1.6-hectare) cooling oasis in the middle of downtown.

Just as the family of publisher Amon G. Carter was Johnson's client on the museum, the Amon Carter Foundation hired the architect and his partner at the time, John Burgee (1933–), to design an outdoor space behind the Fort Worth Convention Center, which was completed in 1968. The convention center and park were two elements in an effort to undo the decades of blight that gave the area the name Hell's Half Acre.

Johnson and Burgee treated the public space as a miniature landscape of mountains, forests, and lakes in three materials: tan-colored concrete, trees (oak, gingko, and gum), and water. Diagonal paths lead from the corners of the irregularly shaped site to the central, polygonal plaza; here, the sounds of the city are buffered by the trees, the artificial mountains, and the sound of water. Befitting the place's name, the three fountains are the main draw, each with a different character, yet each articulated with diagonal lines, a contrast to Johnson's rectilinear sculpture garden at New York's Museum of Modern Art (see 1953). The Sunken Lake, hidden by high walls, is a calm oasis where the pool is rung by rows of cypress trees. The aptly named Dancing Pool features about forty jets shooting water up to create a misty plane above the surface of the water. Most dramatic is the Active Pool, which features water cascading down progressively smaller tiers and fed through twenty narrow channels to a frothy central basin. The designers provided some steps running diagonally to the waterfall for those brave and foolhardy enough to descend to the bottom. Sadly, four people died in the deep pool in June 2004—thirty years after the water gardens were completed and gifted to the city—leading to renovations that raised the floor of the basin to make the pool shallower. Even with warning signs and a memorial for the victims installed, it is still popular to walk the steps to the bottom, where a sense of danger remains.

# 1975 GAS WORKS PARK

## Richard Haag ▸ Seattle, Washington, United States

Seen from Kite Hill, which is topped by a sundial by artists Charles Greening and Kim Lazare, the Gas Works structures sit just beyond the drainage basin that sheds rainwater directly into the lake.

Certainly one characteristic shared by all the artists, architects, and designers who created the hundred landscapes in this book is passion. All of them translated their passion for nature and design into creations that meaningfully mark the earth in ways nature could not have done alone. None approaches the passion of Richard Haag (1923–) at Gas Works Park, since the landscape architect spent twenty years fighting for, designing, and realizing the project—many of those years actually living on the site of the old Gas Works. By doing so, he learned more about the place than anybody else and was able to transform it into something unforeseen.

When Seattle purchased the 20 acres (8 hectares) of the former Seattle Gas Light Company in 1962, six years after the fifty-year-old plant closed, most residents considered it an eyesore and wanted the gasification towers, boiler house, and other industrial buildings demolished and removed. The plant was responsible for polluting Lake Union, whose shoreline it graced, and its noxious smoke, smells, and noise were something the city wanted to move beyond. But Haag, who moved to Seattle from San Francisco in 1958, saw the derelict site differently, in part because he arrived after the plant closed. For him, the industrial structures approached modern art and were the most sacred part of the site, so he set about convincing politicians and residents of their beauty and the need to retain them. He photographed the buildings so they looked like art, threw parties at the site, gave people tours, and then managed to thwart a demolition permit in 1970 and refurbish part of the old blacksmith's shop for his office, where he would also sleep.

With his campaign to save the structures complete, he designed them to be a usable part of the new park: the boiler house became a picnic shelter and the exhauster-compressor building an open-air play barn. (Unfortunately a child was injured playing on the cracking towers, forcing the city to wrap them with a fence.) Opposite the structures he piled the contaminated soil that could not be remediated on-site to create the Great Mound—though breezes earned it the moniker Kite Hill—measuring 45 feet (13.7 meters) tall. A thick layer of clay and topsoil on the hill keeps rain from the contaminated soil beneath, instead shedding it off into Lake Union—an illustration of how Haag's passion extended to the site's ecology.

# 1976 FREEWAY PARK

## Lawrence Halprin ▸ Seattle, Washington, United States

The stepped configuration of the waterfalls and other concrete surfaces has made Freeway Park a popular spot for parkour enthusiasts.

The sight of a park with mature trees spanning across a freeway is a surreal experience thanks to Lawrence Halprin's ingenuity.

Lawrence Halprin (1916–2009) was one of the most innovative landscape architects of the last half of the twentieth century, if for no other reason than an ability to see everything as an opportunity. Even highways, which cut destructive paths across nearly every U.S. downtown following the Federal Aid Highway Act of 1956, were a problem to tame rather than complain about. This assertion was expressed in his 1966 book *Freeways*, which took the high-speed arteries as a fact of urban life, offered solutions, and led to his design of a park spanning a freeway in Seattle.

Freeway Park, as it is aptly named, was originally planned to be a park just east of Interstate 5 where it cut a curved path between downtown on the west and the First Hill neighborhood on the east. The Seattle Park Commission approached Halprin two years after his book was published, but he responded with a proposal to bridge the freeway for an expanded 5-acre (2-hectare) park that would reconnect the neighborhoods that were split by the intrusion of eight lanes of traffic. Yet the park, which opened to the public on July 4, 1976, doesn't simply sit over the freeway like a bridge with trees: it squeezes itself under a north-south overpass, it connects to a convention center that also spans the freeway, it serves as a forecourt for an office tower, and it rests atop a new parking garage.

Simply proposing an overpass park and managing to fit it between the surrounding streets and buildings might have been enough to create a truly innovative park for a city in the age of the automobile, but Halprin gave it loads of character through his handling of surfaces, plantings, and water. Concrete was the obvious choice for supporting the park in its spaghetti-like context, so Halprin used the material throughout: for walkways, steps, planters, plazas, and water features. The concrete surfaces are striated horizontally and vertically throughout, giving the impression that Freeway Park is a carved mass. The trees and other plantings took off in the lush Pacific Northwest climate, so now they cover much of the concrete, but they also give the spaces an appealing intimacy. The handful of fountains and waterfalls spread throughout create moments of emphasis within the park. More important, the falling water drowns out the traffic sounds, leading to the full taming of this stretch of freeway.

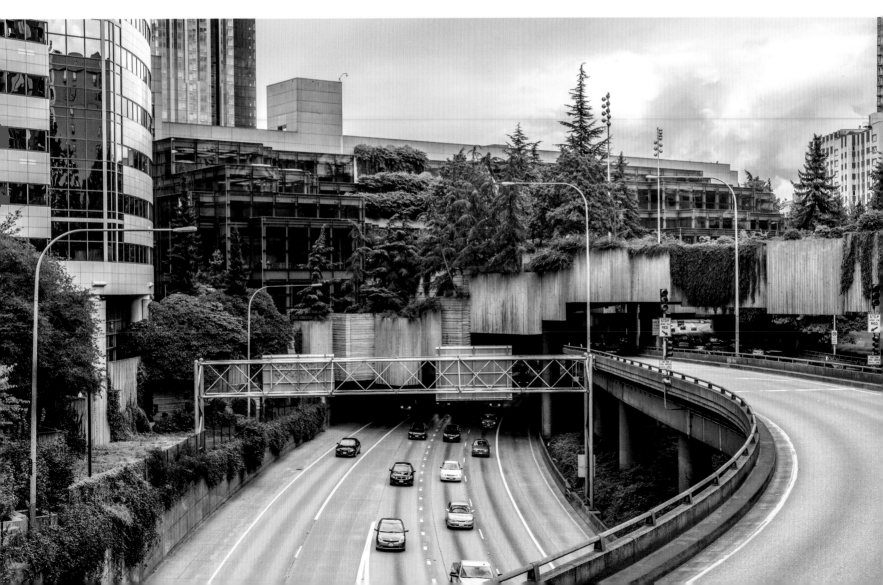

# 1977 OBSERVATORIUM

## Robert Morris ▸ Lelystad, Netherlands

The earthwork's two concentric rings are evident from above, as is the strong integration of the geometric construction with the flat earth.

A V-shaped steel notch set beyond the outer ring was positioned to frame the sunrise on the summer solstice.

As seen with Robert Smithson's *Spiral Jetty* in Utah (see 1970), Land art was a movement born from the American landscape and New York's cultural scene. Regardless of this origin story, Land art was not exclusive to the United States, as Robert Morris's (1931–) *Observatorium* in Holland reveals.

Born in Kansas City, smack in the middle of the United States, Morris had proposed a couple of pieces of Land art—a grass ring for Dallas/Fort Worth International Airport and a serpent mound that would have recalled prehistoric Indian artworks—but neither was built. Then he was invited by curator Wim Beeren—alongside Smithson and numerous American and Dutch artists—to participate in Sonsbeek 71, an art exhibition that embraced large-scale artworks being produced outside of galleries. Many of the artworks were slated for Arnhem's Sonsbeek Park, but Morris searched for a peripheral site for his *Observatorium*, settling on some dunes close to Santpoort in North Holland. Although razed at the end of the exhibition, Morris's earthwork was rebuilt in larger form on an open polder landscape (land reclaimed from the sea through the construction of dikes) in centrally located Flevoland in 1977.

As in the first iteration, *Observatorium* is made up of two concentric rings: an outer ring 200 feet (61 meters) in diameter of three embankments and an inner ring about 80 feet (24 meters) in diameter made from earth piled against a wood stockade. Access to the center is through a triangular portal in the outer ring aligned with one of the four openings in the inner ring. These openings align with the sunrises of the spring and fall equinoxes, and the summer and winter solstices. Three V-shaped notches—two in granite and one in steel—frame the rising sun on those days.

The profiles of the rings recall the dikes that created *Observatorium*'s setting, but its celestial role harkens back to ancient monuments, most notably Stonehenge in England. Whatever the inspiration, Morris wanted the artwork to be about time, the movement of the human body, and the natural setting. The slow merging of the land with *Observatorium* in the forty years since has strengthened the relationship among these three considerations.

# 1978 PIAZZA D'ITALIA

**Charles Moore** ▸ **New Orleans, Louisiana, United States**

Two grinning busts in the likeness of Charles Moore spew water into the basin and add a layer of theatricality to the colorful design.

Postmodern architecture, which came to the fore in the late 1970s and early 1980s, was primarily about buildings rather than landscapes. This makes sense, since its defining trait was the ironic use of historical architectural elements like columns and pediments. But the most successful piece of postmodern architecture, in terms of ironic exuberance and polarizing aesthetics, was a landscape: the fountain Charles Moore (1925–1993) designed for the small Italian community in New Orleans.

Moore, who was working with Urban Innovations Group (UIG) at the time, gained the commission after coming in second place for a competition to design the larger Piazza d'Italia project, which would have included buildings around it. Very little beyond the fountain was built, so what people have encountered since its completion in 1978 is only a partial Piazza d'Italia, open to a parking lot on one side rather than in the middle of what should have become a bustling commercial development. Nevertheless, for Moore it was a particularly exciting project, his first chance to direct the design of a fountain since his doctoral dissertation on water and architecture, and since assisting Lawrence Halprin on a fountain installed at Lovejoy Plaza in Portland, Oregon, in 1965.

Moore and his UIG colleagues approached the design by thinking of the most Italian things possible and coming up with the map of Italy and the Roman orders: Tuscan, Doric, Ionic, Corinthian, and Composite. Alternating lines of slate and light granite crumple up from the circular basin to form the Italian "boot"; Sicily is at the center with a rostrum for St. Joseph's Day festivities, since most of the Italian population of New Orleans traces its heritage to the island. The five orders are arranged along walls and colonnades that follow the circular plan, increasing in complexity from Tuscan near the center to what Moore called the "delicatessen order" at the rear (it frames an opening to a restaurant that never came to be). Moore's creativity with water was rampant: it flows from the "lakes" and "rivers" of the map of Italy into the basin, and a ring of falling water forms the Tuscan columns, to name just two uses. Neon lights round out the colorful postmodern design features of the Piazza d'Italia, which was restored in 2004, a sign that criticism of the design has given way to a reappraisal of the fountain's brazen postmodern manners.

# 1979 ROBSON SQUARE

## Cornelia Hahn Oberlander ▸ Vancouver, British Columbia, Canada

One of Cornelia Hahn Oberlander's most creative contributions to the project was the "stramps" that make an accessible connection between the street and roof gardens.

Located on the edges of residential, commercial, and industrial areas when built, Robson Square sits in the middle of a downtown that boomed in the ensuing decades.

In the middle of the twentieth century there was a tendency for urban planners to create superblocks, whereby streets were removed and blocks were bundled together for large developments, such as civic centers and convention centers. Vancouver was no different with its three-block-long Robson Square, except the project's buildings and landscapes worked together to maintain the blocks, allowing people to pass across and even over them.

In the late 1960s the lack of a civic center in Vancouver was a growing concern, as was the need for a new courthouse. Architect Arthur Erickson's firm was hired to study the impact of a civic and governmental complex on the city's core and then was hired to design the buildings that would sit on the two blocks directly west of the early twentieth-century courthouse the city had outgrown. Around this time a fifty-five-story tower was proposed for the same site, and strong public opposition to it led Erickson to propose what was in effect a tower on its side, spanning across the two blocks. He designed roof gardens bridging Smithe Street on the west, while a tunnel under Robson Street connected the middle block to the old courthouse site on the east. The architect devised schematic plans for the roof gardens, with the Oakland Museum of California (see 1969) as a precedent, but to complete them he turned to landscape architect Cornelia Hahn Oberlander (1921–). The middle and west blocks opened to the public in 1979, though the Vancouver Art Gallery wouldn't move into the old courthouses until 1983.

Oberlander's tasks were as much technical as they were design-related. In regard to the first, she used drip irrigation, which was new at the time, and worked with horticultural expert Raoul Robillard to research the proper growing medium for the more than fifty thousand rooftop shrubs and trees. In terms of design, she proposed a range of spaces and plant types to entice people to ascend the roof gardens and to highlight Erickson's architecture. Among these, an allée of red sunset maples softens the street edge on the north; a huge mound built atop Styrofoam blocks looks like an untamed chunk of nature landed in the city; and a series of waterfalls drowns out the sounds of traffic while serving as part of the buildings' air-conditioning system. The last reveals that the technical and design aspects could merge, even blurring the distinction between building and landscape.

# 1980 ALEXANDRA ROAD PARK

## Janet Jack ▸ London, England

Diagonal paths cut across the long open space to create a series of distinct outdoor "rooms" for play and relaxation.

The five age-specific playgrounds that stretch across the long park are accessed by the zigzag walkways.

The decades after World War II saw cities making numerous attempts at urban renewal, mainly following Le Corbusier's "Towers in a Park" formula. Unfortunately, the landscapes around modern towers often were an afterthought, which led some designers and planners to propose housing schemes that lowered the scale of the buildings and articulated their landscapes as usable spaces. A prime example is Alexandra Road, a housing estate designed by Neave Brown of Camden Council's Architects Department with landscape design by Janet Jack (1934–2016).

In 1965 the London Borough of Camden bought 13.5 acres (5.5 hectares) of land running east-west between the recently completed Ainsworth Estate on the south and the railroad tracks heading to Euston Station on the north. Starting in 1968, Brown designed the housing scheme with five hundred dwellings as three parallel rows of buildings that curved to follow the tracks, with the tallest row—Block A—placed next to the tracks to buffer train noises. A walkway—Rowley Way—sat between Blocks A and B, while the park occupied the 4 acres (1.6 hectares) between Blocks B and C, which were shorter to ensure that the park got plenty of sunlight. Without a program to fill the park, Brown conceptualized the long space as landforms that would give some interest to the otherwise flat site. By the time Jack came on board in 1976, the park's program consisted of five playgrounds, a football pitch, an amphitheater, and a play center building. Jack took Brown's layout—whose landforms were made with fill from excavation for the buildings—and used trees, shrubs, and flowering plants to create comfortable spaces, to shield the spaces from one another and from the housing blocks, and to cut down on the prevailing winds.

The buildings were completed and occupied in 1979 and construction on the landscape wrapped up in 1980. Although Jack designed a low-maintenance landscape, the removal of playground equipment, plantings, and other park features, combined with a lack of maintenance, resulted in a park that was not being used to its fullest potential. So in 2010 a group of residents started a successful bid to fund the park's restoration, which was carried out by J & L Gibbons (landscape design) and Erect Architecture (playground design) and completed in July 2015. Both firms consulted closely with Jack to ensure that the contemporary creations remained true to her original designs.

# 1981 SEASIDE

## Andres Duany, Elizabeth Plater-Zyberk ▸ Seaside, Florida, United States

The Urban Code's restrictions on building heights are relaxed for structures with small footprints, which led to towers grasping for views of the Gulf.

Brick paving, white picket fences, small yards, native landscapes, and front porches all merge to create a distinctly anti-sprawl character.

Seaside, the popular resort community on Florida's Panhandle, is known best for its quaint residential buildings that recall traditional small towns predating America's postwar suburban explosion. This similarity is not a coincidence, since husband-and-wife architects and planners Andres Duany (1949–) and Elizabeth Plater-Zyberk (1950–) saw Seaside as an opportunity to dismantle the norms of suburban sprawl in favor of what came to be known as New Urbanism. Yet the architectural appeal of the town is only half the story, since the real innovation is found in the spaces between the buildings.

Duany and Plater-Zyberk were partners at the Miami firm Arquitectonica when they started working with developer Robert Davis to plan a resort on 80 acres (32 hectares) he inherited on the Gulf Coast. Soon after being hired, the couple left to start their own eponymous firm (DPZ, for short), and then the project shifted toward becoming a full-fledged town, albeit a small one with many vacationers. Client and architects visited and measured small towns in Florida and other parts of the South, leading to the "Urban Code" DPZ developed specifically for Seaside. With input from traditional architect Léon Krier and students at the University of Miami and the University of Notre Dame, the code's breakdown of building types and open space requirements was overlaid onto a plan with streets radiating out from a central open space. Commercial spaces topped by apartments occupied the center, civic buildings were sited prominently on major axes, and the different types of houses filled in the rest of the lots.

Where Seaside, which was "born" in 1981 according to its founder, differs most from American suburbia are the streets, those spaces between buildings given over to cars. Suburbs tend to be made up of culs-de-sac and arterial roads, but Seaside is all through-streets with only one major road—Highway 30A—cutting through town, just like traditional towns more than a half century ago. Driveways and garages are accessed from alleys behind the houses, so the streets are places to walk and bike, and the houses—working with the Urban Code—feature front porches that are meant to engender a sense of community. That *The Truman Show* chose Seaside as its setting shows there is a perceived downside to the nostalgic facades, but that hasn't stopped Seaside from becoming one of the country's most imitated towns—with some of the imitators even surrounding the 8-acre (3 hectacres) original.

# 1982 VIETNAM VETERANS MEMORIAL

## Maya Lin ▸ Washington, DC, United States

Maya Lin's alignment of one wall of the memorial with the Washington Monument is easy to grasp when ascending the path next to the polished granite wall.

From the moment it was dedicated on November 13, 1982, the Vietnam Veterans Memorial has been a popular and powerful site able to elicit strong emotions. That it does so is remarkable given the memorial's minimal, abstract design and the numerous controversies that swirled around the project as it moved from competition to realization.

The memorial process started with the 1979 formation of the Vietnam Veterans Memorial Fund (VVMF), which oversees the Wall, as it's commonly known, to this day. After procuring 2 prominent acres (.8 hectares) on the National Mall, the VVMF held an open, anonymous design competition in 1981. From the more than fourteen hundred entries, the jury decided unanimously on the entry authored by Maya Lin (1959–), then a twenty-one-year-old architecture student at Yale University. That Lin is Chinese American was one source of controversy, but much of the opposition came from veterans and others who wanted acknowledgment for their service and the lives lost to come in the form of a figural representation, such as a statue of soldiers. Lin's design was free of any representation; it was simply two walls— one aligned toward the Lincoln Memorial and one aligned toward the Washington Monument—that were cut into the earth and etched with the names of the more than fifty-eight thousand men and women who lost their lives during the Vietnam War. She arranged the names chronologically so soldiers that served and returned could find their place in the memorial whose tapered walls serve as a timeline of the conflict. Lin referred to the polished black granite, another source of controversy, as dark mirrors rather than as black walls; they are the interface between the living on one side and the departed beyond.

Lin worked with the DC architecture and landscape firm Cooper-Lecky Partnership to bring her poetic design to life as faithfully as possible. But even with a successful translation from drawing to construction, the dissenting voices managed to push through two figural additions to the memorial: a statue with three soldiers, dedicated in 1984, and the Vietnam Women's Memorial, dedicated in 1993 as a group of four female figures. (Thankfully, both are located at a remove from Lin's Wall.) One indication of the ongoing emotional impact of the Wall, versus these later additions, can be seen in the half-size replica that has toured the United States since 1984, bringing Lin's powerful abstraction to even more people.

# 1983 GEOMETRIC GARDENS

## Carl Theodor Sørensen ▸ Birk, Denmark

The narrow, in-between spaces of the Geometric Gardens are as important as the larger spaces formed by the hedges.

Set into a large oval opening in the trees, the Geometric Gardens' tangential "rooms" are approached by diagonal paths.

Clipped trees or hedges are not an uncommon part of historical gardens, such as in the bosquets of baroque parks in Denmark and other European countries. Yet where hedges were lined up traditionally in neat rows or in symmetrical arrangements, in the hands of C. Th. Sørensen (1893–1979) they were a means of expressing geometric complexity and creating memorable experiences.

Designed in 1945 for Vitus Berings Park in Horsens, Denmark, the Geometric Gardens were not realized until 1956, in a small version, and then full-size in 1983, four years after Sørensen's death; the latter for textile manufacturer Aage Damgaard in Herning. The gardens are now part of an assemblage of buildings and open spaces anchored by HEART—Herning Museum of Contemporary Art and the Carl-Henning Pedersen and Else Alfelt Museum. HEART oversees the Geometric Gardens as well as an adjacent sculpture park laid out geometrically by Sørensen as well; the former is set into an oval opening within a forest, while the latter is a larger circular opening where the sculptures occupy small "rooms" along the perimeter.

Unlike the sculpture park, the Geometric Gardens are not accompanied by any art—the landscape design is the art. Clipped hornbeams at a height of 20 to 26 feet (6 to 8 meters) are arranged into nine distinct elements: a line, a circle, an oval, and six polygons with three to eight sides. The line hedge and each side of the polygons are exactly 33 feet (10 meters) long. These shapes are positioned tangentially to one another in ascending order, accompanied by a small circle and large oval on either side. Openings cut into the hedges allow visitors to move freely about the labyrinthine composition, including the in-between spaces, making it reminiscent of Sørensen's Nærum Allotment Gardens (see 1948).

The designer originally called the project the Musical Garden. His composition of eight spaces following geometric and numerical arrangements weds the garden to music, most overtly in relation to the octaves. There is something musical about the rhythmic experience of moving through the garden and the sheer joy of getting lost within the green walls open to the sky.

# 1984 TANNER FOUNTAIN

## Peter Walker ▸ Cambridge, Massachusetts, United States

*Unlike most fountains, Tanner Fountain overlaps grass as well as a few trees (pin oaks), the latter providing shade around the rocks and mist.*

Tanner Fountain is a fountain unlike any that came before. It has two main ingredients that define public fountains—water in the center and a perimeter for seating—but the fountain does not incorporate a basin, the water is more vapor than liquid, and the boulders that make up the seats allow people to walk into its center. By departing from historical precedents, Peter Walker (1932–) created a piece of art that masquerades as a fountain.

Walker was working at the SWA Group, the firm he cofounded in 1957 (he started his eponymous practice in 1983, one year before the fountain's completion), when he was commissioned by Harvard University president Derek Bok to design a fountain that could not be turned into a planter by weary maintenance workers, as had happened previously on campus when other fountains broke down. Walker's basinless fountain—a first of its kind—deterred such a transformation, but it also called for some technical assistance to make the mechanically complex design a reality. Walker worked with fountain consultant Richard Chaix to develop the number, configuration, and type of spray heads to achieve a waterfall-like mist in the center of the fountain during most of the year, and then he turned to environmental artist Joan Brigham for assistance on its winter state, when the stones are shrouded with steam from the university's heating plant.

Walker and Bok considered ten sites on campus and in Harvard Square, and in the end the fountain was sited near the entrance to the Josep Lluís Sert–designed Science Center as part of a new plaza just north of Harvard Yard. On a plot of land that is part grass and part asphalt, Walker placed the 60-foot-diameter (18-meter) circular fountain so it overlaps half of these surfaces. Thirty-two spray nozzles and lights occupy the center of the circle, while 159 granite boulders gathered from farms in the region radiate randomly outward. Recalling the standing stones of Avebury and Stonehenge, and bringing to mind the Big Bang, the ever-changing effect of Tanner Fountain's mist and boulders invites multiple interpretations, but in the end a pleasing sense of mystery prevails—fitting for a design that is as poetic as it is one-of-a-kind.

# 1985 DONALD M. KENDALL SCULPTURE GARDENS

## Edward Durell Stone Jr., Russell Page ▸ Purchase, New York, United States

To best place the sculptures and surrounding plantings (Henry Moore's *Double Oval* visible here), Russell Page had full-scale mockups of the sculptures made before they were put into place.

Edward Durell Stone Jr. designed the headquarters as interconnected pavilions, resulting in courtyards that Page filled with his signature formal touches.

The sculpture gardens that surround the headquarters of PepsiCo in New York's Westchester County are the product of two landscape architects spanning more than fifteen years. Although a corporate campus, the Donald M. Kendall Sculpture Gardens are notable for being open to the public and as a beautiful setting for art.

Pepsi made the move to the suburbs from New York's Park Avenue in 1970, after CEO Donald M. Kendall found a 122-acre (49-hectare) former polo club surrounded by old-growth forest. The beverage company was not alone in the suburban exodus, as numerous corporations made the move to new campuses in this part of New York and nearby Connecticut in the late 1960s and early 1970s. Regardless, Kendall was concerned about drops in employee satisfaction arising from the move, so he surrounded the headquarters with a lush park dotted with modern art. Architect Edward Durell Stone was responsible for the low-slung building made up of seven interconnected structures, so naturally the commission for the surrounding landscape went to his son, Edward Durell Stone Jr. (1932–2009). He designed a ring road and long strips of parking that followed it; this required employees to walk across the sculpture garden to get to the office, something Kendall liked. Excavation work on the building revealed an on-site spring, so Stone placed an artificial lake at the southern end of the site, a feature that remains a key part of the landscape.

Changes began in 1981 when Kendall brought on the great gardener Russell Page (1906–1985) to carry out what became his last commission; Page worked on the garden up until his death in 1985. He considered the landscape he was given to be bland (needless to say, Stone and Page's working relationship on the project was short) and, although he didn't share Kendall's taste in modern art, he introduced hundreds of plantings to complement the sculptures as well as the Golden Path, an amber-colored loop that traversed the landscape and delivered visitors to each sculpture. Like Storm King Art Center (see 1960), many of the forty-five artworks are large and work best in open spaces against a backdrop of trees, so a number of Page's more delicate contributions are closer to the building, most notably a small formal garden with three lily ponds. The sculpture garden reopened in spring 2017 after a five-year campus renovation.

# 1986 BLOEDEL RESERVE GARDENS

## Richard Haag ▸ Bainbridge Island, Washington, United States

The Moss Garden, originally called the Anteroom by Richard Haag, transitions between the current Japanese Garden and Haag's Reflection Garden.

The low water table of Bainbridge Island means the pool caps the groundwater that is just below its surface.

Before he created the famous Gas Works Park (see 1975), before he moved to Seattle to found the landscape architecture department at the University of Washington, and before he worked for Lawrence Halprin in San Francisco, Richard Haag (1923–) spent two years in Kyoto studying the city's great Zen gardens on a Fulbright Scholarship. This experience gave him an understanding of these traditional gardens that went deep, well beyond the mere appearances of dry rock gardens, moss gardens, and the like. It made him ideally suited to create a trio of Eastern gardens with a Western dialect for timber giant Prentice Bloedel on his 160-acre (49-hectare) estate on Bainbridge Island near Seattle.

Of the three linked gardens that Haag crafted at Bloedel Reserve between 1969 and 1986, only two remain: the Moss Garden and the Reflection Garden. The Garden of Planes, which would have been the first garden encountered in a stroll through the three gardens, now features a traditional dry rock garden (aptly going by the name Japanese Garden) by Koichi Kawana in place of Haag's avant-garde creation. Featuring a rectangular landform with a shallow pyramid and an inverted pyramid surrounded by undulating mounds (these remain in place), the garden was designed for maximum impact, aimed at experiencing satori, or Zen enlightenment, on one's first step in.

While the Garden of Planes shocked, the Moss Garden—Haag's last creation at Bloedel Reserve and the next in the linked trio—went to the other extreme, calming visitors as they strolled through a dark, almost primordial forest. Haag's hand here is light, to the extent that the Moss Garden doesn't look designed at all. Beside the path are more than forty-five different kinds of mosses and lichens that combine with the trees and other plants to heighten smell over the other senses.

The last garden, the Reflection Garden, was completed first. When Haag was hired his first task was to address his predecessor Thomas Church's Canal Pond. Church had designed formal landscapes around the main house that remain, but for Bloedel the Canal Pond was murky so Haag completed Church's design by enclosing the long rectangular pool with the simplest of means: a 12-foot (3.6-meter) wall of yew hedges and a lawn in between. With its still water and the reflections of the surrounding fir and cedar trees, the last of the three gardens is a moment of release—maybe even of satori.

# 1987 PARC DE LA VILLETTE

## Bernard Tschumi ▸ Paris, France

Most of the park's northern half is occupied by the Cité des Sciences et de l'Industrie, whose spherical cinema reaches toward the red *folies*.

The Canal de l'Ourcq splits the park into northern and southern halves. The southern half, on the left, features an elevated walkway strung along the grid of *folies*.

Deconstructivist architecture was a short-lived movement of sorts in the late 1980s and early 1990s in which the forms of Russian Constructivism coincided with Jacques Derrida's philosophy of deconstruction to shape a few select parts of the built environment. The earliest and most notable application of these two aspects of the style took place in Paris, with French-Swiss architect Bernard Tschumi's (1944–) 1983 competition-winning design for the 125-acre (50-hectare) Parc de la Villette, located on the site of former slaughterhouses in the 19th arrondissement in the northeast corner of the city. It was fitting that his innovative design was selected from the 476 entries, since the city was aiming for a completely new type of urban park, a park for the twenty-first century.

In response to the competition brief's call for a complex program of cultural and entertainment facilities alongside inventive gardens, Tschumi developed a plan that superimposed three distinct systems: points, lines, and surfaces. The points consist of a grid of thirty-five unique red *folies* whose forms resemble exploded cubes and recall the early twentieth-century drawings of Russian architect Yakov Chernikhov; the lines are made up of covered walkways, a promenade of gardens, and allées of trees; and the surfaces are devoted to paved areas and expansive lawns. Relating to Derrida's philosophy, which espouses the meaninglessness of language arising from the multiple interpretations of any text, Tschumi designed the park's signature *folies* and other elements without any regard for function: the city and its residents had to determine their uses over time. In the years since the park ceremoniously opened on October 12, 1987 (only partially, the whole wasn't completed until 1998), it has served as a venue for concerts and performances as well as sports and recreation.

In Tschumi's role as the park's master planner, a number of pieces were designed by others, particularly the themed gardens strung along the curvilinear path he coined the Cinematic Promenade. Most notable are the bamboo garden designed by Alexandre Chemetoff, a dense, sunken landscape traversed by catwalks, and Bernhard Leitner's sound garden (in a corner of the bamboo garden), a circular space of concrete, water, and prerecorded audio. Although avant-garde in execution, these gardens lend some tradition to a park that was without precedent.

# 1988 KIKAR LEVANA

## Dani Karavan ▸ Tel Aviv, Israel

The tower atop this highest hill in Tel Aviv affords westward views toward the center of Tel Aviv and the Mediterranean beyond.

There are few environmental artists as prolific and enduring as Dani Karavan, who was born in Israel in 1930. His diverse output of sculptural works built upon Platonic geometries grew in scale from the *Negev Monument* (1968) in Beersheba, Israel, to the 2-mile (3.2-kilometer) *Axe Majeur* in Cergy-Pontoise, France, which he has been working on since 1980. A standout is *Kikar Levana* (White Square), which sits in the middle of Edith Wolfson Park in southeastern Tel Aviv.

Karavan started working on the project in 1977 when Zvi Dekel, cofounder of Tichnun Nof Landscape Architects, invited the artist to create three playgrounds in the park he had just finished work on. Edith Wolfson Park, marked by groves of sycamore trees, is notable for being the highest point in Tel Aviv. Accordingly, a luxury restaurant was planned for the highest point within the park, but Karavan proposed an observatory that *everyone* could access and enjoy. His commission shifted to a sculptural square, which he completed in 1988 when he returned to the city after nine years in Italy and France.

Karavan looked to the park and the city for inspiration. Confronted with an existing steel alarm tower that had to stay, he encased it in white concrete and installed wind flutes. Park goers can ascend the tower for panoramic views of the city or they can climb in, on, or around the other geometric features: a pyramid with one half of one side removed, a sunken square amphitheater, and a narrow stair aligned with the channel bisecting the square. Two other elements relate to the park: a dome cut in two with an olive tree in its center and a round depression at the southern edge of the square. While the dome appears to encase nature, much like the white concrete does the same to the alarm tower, the last feature, the depression, continues into the park as a valley, a subtle link between the white concrete sculpture and the green park.

More than just a contrast in its green surroundings, the bright white sculpture relates to Tel Aviv's designation as the "White City," which arose from its density of modern, International Style architecture created in the 1930s to 1950s. The buildings from this period are at a remove from the sculpture, but the orientation of the sculpture's plinth points toward the city's historical center—from one White City to another.

# 1989 CANADIAN CENTRE FOR ARCHITECTURE GARDEN

**Melvin Charney** ▸ **Montreal, Canada**

Classical, religious, and even industrial buildings were mined as allegorical sources in the creation of the columns that occupy the eastern half of the garden.

The western half of the garden is a softer landscape that is highlighted by a ruinlike reconstruction of the 1874 house the Canadian Centre for Architecture calls home.

Although the Canadian Centre for Architecture (CCA), founded by Phyllis Lambert in 1979, is known primarily for its extensive research collection and intelligent exhibitions, it's no surprise that the institution has its own piece of landscape architecture. After all, architecture, in the widest sense of the term, comprises buildings, landscapes, and their context, in this case the western end of downtown Montreal. The garden's design illustrates these three aspects of architecture, in turn making it a suitable companion to the building that houses the museum's collection.

Five years before Lambert founded the CCA she bought the 1874 Shaughnessy House, a remnant of the area's rich residential past that was named a historic site the same year. Residential high-rises and highway construction had maligned much of the area's historical fabric in the 1970s, such that the neighborhood around the CCA became Shaughnessy Village, in honor of its landmark survivor. In the mid-1980s Lambert started working with architect Peter Rose on the CCA's new building that would wrap around and incorporate the old house, and in 1986 the City of Montreal gave her land across Boulevard René-Lévesque for a garden that would integrate art and architecture. Artist-architect Melvin Charney (1935–2012) won the 1987 competition for the 2-acre (.8-hectare) plot of land with sculpture and landscape that reveal the history of the site, much of it previously erased.

Charney saw the garden, sitting directly across from the CCA but disconnected from it by eight lanes of traffic, as much for the neighborhood as for the museum. The design splits itself into two different experiences: the section near the road provides shade and lawn for strolling or sitting, while the hardscape sculpture plaza looks out beyond the highway to the St. Lawrence River in the distance. Charney layered historical references throughout the design: an apple tree orchard harkens back to nineteenth-century farms; parallel stone walls projecting from the lawn recall the area's cadastral grid of land division; a partial mirror reconstruction of the Shaughnessy Houses's facade reminds people of the area's historical residential streetscapes; and a series of allegorical columns piece together architectural features from older buildings, many demolished. It is a highly intellectualized, even esoteric landscape that benefits from its dramatic setting, poised between Mount Royal and the river, and across from Lambert's CCA, which continues to provoke.

# 1990 JARDÍN DE CACTUS

## César Manrique ▸ Guatiza, Lanzarote, Spain

Much like the Desert Garden at the Huntington Botanical Gardens (see 1919), the Cactus Garden is a repository of thousands of desert plants artistically arranged.

The windmill that César Manrique found on the site and fixed up gives an elevated view of the garden as well as the village of Guatiza in the distance.

The first cactus that visitors encounter at the Jardín de Cactus (Cactus Garden) in the village of Guatiza isn't alive—it's a metal sculpture that sits on a circular base in the middle of a parking lot. It marks the last creation of artist César Manrique (1919–1992). Although the cartoonish sculpture serves as a sign that people of any language or nationality can understand, it also readies visitors for a garden that is as much about art as it is about cacti.

Manrique was born on Lanzarote, the easternmost of the Canary Islands, and he returned to live there in the 1960s after he studied (both art and architecture) and lived in Madrid, and then lived in New York for a brief time. The paintings he made there were abstract, but they expressed the volcanic landscape of his home island, foreshadowing his return. Upon his return, his artworks grew in size and in scope, encompassing landscapes that he described as "art-nature/nature-art." These exhibited a renewed appreciation of Lanzarote but also a desire to bring tourists to the island. He founded the César Manrique Foundation in 1983 to further this aim. Since his death, the artist's home in the village of Taro de Tahíche has served as the foundation's headquarters.

If the most important art produced by Manrique occurred after he returned to Lanzarote, the Cactus Garden is clearly his masterpiece and probably the greatest creation on the island. Located on the site of an abandoned stone quarry that he found in the early 1970s while working on a guidebook of the island's native architecture, he started transforming the hole full of dirt into a hole full of cacti in 1976, finally completing it in 1990 and opening it to the public the same year. Punctuated by a windmill on the eastern edge, the entrance is located opposite it on the west, where Manrique placed a small archway (reached from the parking lot) and a small domed structure made from rough quarry lava, echoes of the native buildings he documented. A few steps past the structure and the whole garden is revealed, with the windmill and restaurant below it luring people across the expanse. New staggered terraces describe the place's former use, while stone pathways meander about islands with large rocks, ponds, and more than seven thousand plants from around eleven hundred species of cacti. The whole is rough, befitting the volcanic island, but meticulously planned, from the arrangement of plants to the cactus-shaped bathroom door handles.

# 1991 BRYANT PARK

**Laurie Olin** ▸ **New York City, United States**

Two levels of stacks with 3.2 million volumes sit out of sight below the park's central lawn, an ingenious solution to the library's space problems in the 1980s.

The park's stately London plane trees shade the promenades alongside the large planting beds filled with low ground cover.

First-time visitors to Bryant Park—the half block of open space between Times Square and Grand Central in Midtown Manhattan—would be forgiven for thinking of the park as a historical landscape. With its stately London plane trees and wrought iron fences, the 9-acre (3.6-hectare) park appears contemporaneous with the adjacent 1911 New York Public Library designed by Carrère and Hastings. Yet the park is actually a late twentieth-century reuse of a park from the 1930s.

A park on this Midtown block dates back to the 1840s, following the completion of the Croton Reservoir on its eastern half. Reservoir Square, as it was called, gave way to a formal park in 1871 that was renamed for William Cullen Bryant, a poet and editor who was instrumental in the creation of Central Park. The reservoir came down in 1897 and the library went up in its place, but in the early decades of last century the park already was plagued by problems and neglect, even serving as a dumping ground. New York "power broker" Robert Moses endorsed a competition in 1934 to redesign the park with a French Beaux-Arts plan, and it was this plan that got landmarked forty years later, when the park happened to see a rise in muggings and drug use. The renovation of the Carrère and Hastings edifice in 1979 spurred efforts to renovate the adjacent park, a job the Bryant Park Corporation (a nonprofit that still manages the publicly owned park) gave to landscape architect Laurie Olin (1938–) of the Philadelphia firm Hanna/Olin.

Olin followed the lead of influential author and urban advocate William H. Whyte, who believed design strategies could reverse the park's problems: remove the iron fencing and thick shrubs at the perimeter, add more access points, and restore the park's notable design features. Minus the fencing, which stayed in place due to preservationists, Olin incorporated Whyte's suggestions, while also adding two levels of library stacks below the central lawn. Today, the park is a hive of activity at any time of the day or day of the year, due in part to Olin's porous and historically true design, but also the numerous kiosks and programs that occur there: lunchtime concerts, summer movies on the lawn, a children's carousel, a wintertime ice rink, and a holiday market, to name a few. With so many crowds, the crime and neglect are a distant memory.

# 1992 PARC ANDRÉ CITROËN

**Alain Provost, Gilles Clément** ▸ **Paris, France**

Toward the end of the century, as factories departed for the periphery, many cities had the opportunity to transform large-scale industrial land into parkland. Paris had three such sites within its borders, two of them in this book: Parc de la Villette, on former slaughterhouses in the 19th arrondissement (see 1987), and Parc André Citroën, where Citroën once made cars in the 15th arrondissement.

André Citroën's factory sat on the Left Bank of the River Seine from 1915 to 1974, first churning out weapons and ammunition and then producing the Torpedo, the DS, and other automobiles. After moving to Aulnay-sous-Bois on the city's fringes, Paris bought up the factory's 57 acres (23 hectares) to build a hospital, housing, office buildings, and a large 35-acre (14-hectare) park at its core. A competition was held under Mayor Jacques Chirac in 1985 for a park "for the twenty-first century," but instead of one clear winner, two similar-enough schemes were selected and then combined to create the park's final design. One team was made up of landscape architect Alain Provost (1938–) with architects Jean-Paul Viguier and Jean-François Jordy, while the other team consisted of landscape architect Gilles Clément (1943–) with architect Patrick Berger.

Each scheme had a large central rectangle, but in Provost's scheme it was a sloping lawn and in Clément's scheme it was a series of gardens. In the final design, the lawn, cut by a diagonal path at one corner, occupies the center, alongside a canal punctuated by a series of stone guard houses designed by Viguier. On the opposite side of the lawn are Clément's gardens: five Serial Gardens (one for each of the senses) and the Garden of Movement, which is located at the northwestern end of the diagonal path and designed to be wilder than anything else in the park. The southeastern end of the diagonal is home to the Black Garden, which extends out into the surrounding neighborhood similar to the White Garden located northeast of the central lawn.

Some changes have occurred since the park opened to great fanfare in September 1992: it was connected to the Seine by a walkway tucked between a roadway and railroad; it received a balloon attraction at the western end of the lawn; and its maintenance tumbled. The last of these means many of Clément's gardens have become as wild as the Garden of Movement, even though they weren't intended to be.

# 1993 PARQUE ECOLÓGICO XOCHIMILCO

**Mario Schjetnan** ▸ **Mexico City, Mexico**

Seen from the water tower, a winding path with pergola leads visitors past the ecological park's demonstration gardens and toward the boat launch for exploring the historic landscape by gondola.

Every landscape design must confront history. The condition of a site, after all, is the accumulation of historical events and processes up to that point. Of course, some places are more laden with cultural baggage than others, forcing designers to act as preservationists as well as designers. One of the most dramatic sites in this regard is the Parque Ecológico Xochimilco (Xochimilco Ecological Park), which is made up partly of pre-Aztec *chinampas* (agricultural islands) that were added to the UNESCO World Heritage List in 1987.

Ten years before that designation, Mario Schjetnan (1945–) started the firm Grupo de Diseño Urbano (GDU) with degrees in both architecture and landscape architecture. His interests in cultural history, social concerns, and environmental restoration made his firm ideally suited for the new Xochimilco Ecological Park, located on 740 acres (300 hectares) adjacent to the network of one-thousand-year-old canals and artificial agricultural islands that cover an area ten times as large. Schjetnan served as principle designer for the park and as an outside consultant for the restoration of the UNESCO site. Work on the latter consisted of the creation of sewage facilities to treat polluted surface water and reservoirs to control storm water runoff entering the site from the surrounding urban areas, the dredging of canals to make them navigable by recreational gondolas, and the rebuilding of the islands with an eye toward returning some of them to agricultural uses.

As designed by Schjetnan, the new park, completed in 1993 and located north and west of the *chinampas*, is split into three zones: the ecological park with its large, 133-acre (54-hectare) lake, a sports park with playing fields, and a flower market with eighteen hundred stalls that picks up on the meaning of Xochimilco as "place where flowers are grown." The last two are located west of a wide boulevard and linked to the ecological park on the east by pedestrian bridges. A visitor center and water tower (both designed by Schjetnan) serve as a launching point for exploring the ecological park on foot or by boat. Next to these structures is a row of stone aqueducts that release recycled and cleansed water into the lake, a body of water that regulates the water level in the historic canal system. With the lake, old and new are inextricably linked—the new helping to maintain the old and the old giving the new a reason to exist.

# 1994 IGUALADA CEMETERY

## Enric Miralles, Carme Pinós ▸ Igualada, Spain

With its trees and creative paving scheme, the cemetery feels like a park, but one where visitors happen to be strolling through a city of the dead.

An upper level with angled benches extends the parklike feeling, inviting people to sit down and stay for a while.

Like fellow Catalan Antoni Gaudí, Enric Miralles (1955–2000)—both with his first and second wives/partners Carme Pinós (1954–) and Benedetta Tagliabue (1963–)—had an instantly recognizable style that he brought to bear on buildings and landscapes. In terms of the latter, he and Pinós applied curved lines, angled concrete walls, and jagged overhangs to the archery range for Barcelona's Olympics in 1992. Soon after, they carried out similar marks in the landscape of Igualada, an industrial area on the outskirts of Barcelona, for a cemetery bordering the Riera d'Òdena.

Miralles and Pinós won a competition for the cemetery with a Z-shaped plan that began where the road lined with industrial buildings ended, just shy of the river. Only the first leg of the "Z," completed in 1994, was carried out; likewise, a chapel embedded in the mountain sits unfinished, temporary bracing holding up the roof. Unlike a traditional cemetery that is set off from its surroundings by a perimeter wall, the Igualada Cemetery is shaped like a valley, with the landscape extending over the graves. Only a pivoted gate made from rusted steel reinforcing bars signals the buried cemetery beyond.

Once through the gate, the path is straight and descends gradually. Concrete walls with crypts line both sides of the promenade, their profiles sloping inward and outward and capped by cantilevered concrete prows. The gravel path with its random insertions of railroad ties (dead trees) and living trees culminates in an elliptical space lined with gabion walls. Here the visitor is completely enveloped by the cemetery and the departed lining its sunken spaces. From there the second leg of the "Z" would have started, but only a second layer of concrete walls with crypts was created along one side, accessed by openings pierced into the gabion walls. The view of the cemetery and the surroundings from the second level illustrates how Miralles and Pinós created a cemetery that is *of* its site: the sloped walls echo the banks of the river and the rough surfaces are at home with its industrial neighbors.

# 1995 SITE OF REVERSIBLE DESTINY—YORO PARK

## Arakawa and Madeline Gins ▸ Yoro, Japan

This view of the center of the Elliptical Bowl, taken around the time the park opened, reveals the numerous "landing sites" that are now shrouded by mature trees.

The husband-and-wife artists Shusaku Arakawa (1936–2010) and Madeline Gins (1941–2014) staked out a unique artistic position that merged art, architecture, landscape, and text toward the theoretical—if impossible—abolishment of human mortality. Although the couple worked in a variety of media—film, poetry, drawing, computer rendering, painting, and sculpture—full-scale environments were the ideal canvas for their ideas. At Yoro Park, in Japan's Gifu Prefecture, they realized their largest construction, one of the best places for grasping how they conceptualized immortality.

A hint as to Arakawa (he was known professionally by his surname) and Gins's intention can be found in the name of the park as they called it: Site of Reversible Destiny. The couple saw humans as inhabiting "architectural bodies" linked with surroundings that would activate them, and which people would in turn activate. The interface of this reciprocal existence between people and their surroundings was called a "landing site," and the more complex and challenging the site the more it would stimulate the body and postpone the inevitable—death. Therefore, the reversing of destiny would be aided by uneven walking surfaces, tight spaces, low clearances, lots of color, and furnishings that were difficult to figure out. The Site of Reversible Destiny is full of these on 4.5 acres (1.8 hectares) of land in one corner of Yoro Park.

Arakawa and Gins's experience park basically consists of two parts: the Critical Resemblances House, a "house" in that it has furnishings and fixtures, but these are sliced up and set among atypical walls, floors, and ceilings; and the Elliptical Bowl, which is walled off at its perimeter and made up of a mix of unexpected plantings and hardscape surfaces (including a map of Japan) in between. After a visit to the house, visitors can traverse the bowl's wall via narrow walkways that afford views into the park as well as those of the distant Nagoya skyline. They can descend to areas the artists labeled with esoteric names, such as the Landing Site Processing Zone and the Reversible Destiny Redoubled Effort Zone, culminating in the Destiny House at the central low point of the bowl. While the Site of Reversible Destiny won't turn back time or halt death, a visit to it just might affect how one perceives his or her surroundings, full as it is of artistic potential and obstacles for traversing.

# 1996 LES JARDINS DE L'IMAGINAIRE

## Kathryn Gustafson ▸ Terrasson-Lavilledieu, France

An amphitheater is set up for views of the Vézère Valley and the historic town of Terrasson-Lavilledieu across the river.

The water fountain echoes the Rights of Man Square built in Évry, France, in the early 1990s, which Kathryn Gustafson boasts as the first flexible space with water jets.

At their root, all gardens are products of the imagination. They exist first as ideas—of how to shape the landscape in a way that distinguishes it from the natural surroundings—and then become a reality for people to enjoy. But the aptly named Jardins de l'Imaginaire (Gardens of the Imagination) in France's Aquitaine region aim to stimulate the senses and provoke the minds of visitors so they depart with a new way of looking at things.

Luring visitors was the impetus of creating the gardens; Terrasson-Lavilledieu mayor Pierre Delmon saw too many motorists pass through town on the way to and from Bordeaux without stopping. Following a competition, he hired the team led by landscape architect Kathryn Gustafson (1951–), who was born in the United States but trained and worked in France. Their scheme, "Fragments of the History of Gardens," consisted of a series of smaller experiential installations that were based on traditional gardens but given contemporary form. Built on former agricultural terraces near the Vézère River, the intuitive interpretations of historical designs were nevertheless rooted in the town's landscape and its unique sense of place.

A visit to the gardens begins with the walk from town, where a parallel channel of water hints at the role of this element throughout. Thirteen gardens are experienced through a more or less counterclockwise path across the curving terraces. A golden ribbon winding its way around trees in the Elementary Gardens makes it clear that Gustafson was not afraid to incorporate unnatural elements, a sentiment echoed by some atypical weather vanes found in the Axis of the Winds and metal armatures encountered in the Rose Garden. Architect Ian Ritchie designed a stone-and-glass greenhouse that leans against the hills and provides space for exhibitions, research, and a place to sip some tea.

Yet it's the manipulation of water, particularly at the eastern end of the gardens, that is most dramatic and effective: a stepped channel cutting a path across the landscape and stone steps cascading with water lead to a fountain with Gustafson's signature jets of water—one hundred twenty of them. What was once a source for agricultural irrigation is now a source of sensuous delight—more imaginative than utilitarian.

# 1997 CENTRAL GARDEN

## Robert Irwin ▸ Los Angeles, California, United States

Richard Meier's buildings atop the ridge take on a new reality when seen from across the maze pool of the *Central Garden*.

In 1997, the year architect Frank Gehry completed a branch of the Guggenheim Museum on the banks of the Nervión river in Bilbao, Spain, Richard Meier wrapped up the Getty Center (now The Getty), a $1 billion cultural acropolis on 110 acres (44.5 hectares) overlooking downtown Los Angeles. Of these two high-profile, attention-getting projects that dominated the headlines that year, Meier's hilltop creation—thirteen years in the making—is the more unrelenting: its off-white, metal, and stone facades exhibit the strict geometries that overlay the entire six-building project. Artist Robert Irwin's (1928–) *Central Garden*, a separate art commission, is the campus's antithesis: a soft and colorful creation.

Meier designed the campus along two axes that flare out in plan, from the tram stop that delivers people to the site on the north to the Pacific and downtown views on the south. Stone plazas with the occasional oak tree and water feature sit between the buildings, but at the southern end, in the opening between the two axes, sits Irwin's garden. The artist was given the commission about halfway through the project, a couple of years after Meier's design was approved. Irwin reintroduced the natural canyon that Meier filled with a terrace in his scheme. Below it Irwin filled a bowl with grasses, shrubs, trees, and a maze of flowers in a pool fed by a stream—nary a hard surface or straight line in sight. The forced collaboration was strained, but twenty years after the completion of the campus and 3-acre (1.2-hectare) garden the two are antithetical but inseparable pieces of the place. It's difficult to imagine one without the other.

The contrast between Meier's and Irwin's approaches is pronounced where they meet. At the southern end of Meier's plazas is a fountain—straight as an arrow—that ends in a circular basin; below it is Irwin's rocky stream that winds its way to the pool and its maze of azaleas. A path zigzags across the brook lined with London plane trees and ends at a terrace with "trees" made from steel rebar and covered with colorful bougainvillea. These are the most overtly artistic pieces in a garden that relies on its selection of plants and articulation of materials (stone and wood, mainly) for effect. Irwin worked with a slew of experts so the whole was executed nearly flawlessly, like a life-size canvas where nature is the paint.

# 1998 IL GIARDINO DEI TAROCCHI

## Niki de Saint Phalle ▸ Garavicchio, Italy

The stacked *Magician* and *High Priestess* preside over the pool, in the middle of which sits *The Wheel of Fortune* made by Jean Tinguely.

Sixteenth-century Renaissance gardens, like Villa d'Este and Villa Lante with their clipped hedges, fountains, and axial arrangements, are what Italy is known for in the history of landscape design. At about the same time as these influential gardens, Count Pier Francesco Orsini brought the writings of Virgil and Dante to life in the grotesque forms of the Sacro Bosco of Bomarzo, known as the Park of the Monsters. It's no surprise that, four hundred years later, artist Niki de Saint Phalle (1930–2002) looked to what Orsini did—as well as to kindred creations like Antoni Gaudí's Park Güell—when she embarked upon creating her own significant mark on the Italian landscape: Il Giardino dei Tarocchi (The Tarot Garden).

Saint Phalle was encouraged to take up painting after suffering a mental breakdown in her twenties, advice that would change her life. In the early 1960s she came to attention with her "shooting paintings" and "Nanas." One Nana work exhibited in Stockholm in 1966, done in collaboration with the artist and her future husband Jean Tinguely, invited museumgoers inside the womb of a huge reclining woman through her open legs; it was controversial, yet it foreshadowed her Tarot Garden in Tuscany. After a friend offered her 14 acres (5.6 hectares) of hilltop land near the Mediterranean in the late 1970s, Saint Phalle erected one of the first of the eventual twenty-two Tarot structures: *The Empress*, a busty Sphinx that Saint Phalle lived in for a time—bedroom in one breast, kitchen in the other. Although the artist wrote that the Tarot Garden would not be finished in her lifetime, it opened to the public in May 1998, when a visitor center designed by architect Mario Botta was completed.

The giant, colorful Tarot figures were made from welded steel frames that were wrapped in wire mesh, sprayed with plaster, and then covered with mosaics. Great care was taken to protect the site's olive trees during construction; later, Mediterranean plants were added to keep the garden distinctly Italian. The Sphinx and other prominent figures, such as the *Magician* and *High Priestess*, serve as a backdrop to the central fountain, an otherworldly mirage at the end of a curving, tree-lined path. Although a product of a distinctly artistic vision, Saint Phalle's garden melds carefully into the landscape, creating a dialogue between art and nature that is as crucial as the Italian creations centuries before.

# 1999 JARDÍ BOTÀNIC DE BARCELONA

**Carlos Ferrater, Josep Lluís Canosa, Bet Figueras** ▸ **Barcelona, Spain**

A key element of the second phase reworked one corner of the garden into a multipurpose plaza with tiered seating.

The Mediterranean zones are arranged in plan but also elevation, with trees on the high slopes and shrubs and other plants down low.

Botanical gardens—gardens devoted to the scientific study of plants—are commonly believed to have started in sixteenth-century Italy, but some historians, most notably John Harvey, find their roots in eleventh-century Islamic Spain, in gardens that contained plants from expeditions to Italy and North Africa. This Iberian embrace of botanical research extends to the present, notably in the Jardí Botànic de Barcelona (Botanical Garden of Barcelona), which was created as a container for flora from the Mediterranean basin and four other Mediterranean zones around the world: California, Chile, South Africa, and Australia.

In 1989 an interdisciplinary team led by architects Carlos Ferrater (1944–) and Josep Lluís Canosa (date unknown) and landscape architect Bet Figueras (1957–2010) won an international competition to design the new botanical garden on a northern slope of Barcelona's Montjuïc hill. The competition arose since the facilities built for the 1992 Olympics adversely affected the nearby Jardí Botànic Històric from the 1930s, which was built on an old quarry (eventually it was restored and reopened in 2003). The site for the Jardí Botànic de Barcelona, opposite the Olympic Stadium, was used as a dump from the 1960s to the 1980s. Instead of leveling the site in a tabula rasa treatment, the team opted for a strategy that respected the site's topography. A triangular grid laid over the entire site created the order for the botanical garden, and design software was used to determine the footprints for the five Mediterranean zones as well as the layout of the walkways, the distribution of infrastructure, and the location of buildings. An expansion completed in 2008 reorganized work spaces and expanded landscape features, the latter following the original design's fractal principles.

Although the plantings have obscured much of the triangulated definition of the landscape in the years since the garden's opening in 1999, the underlying geometry is overtly expressed in many areas by concave and convex retaining walls faced in COR-TEN steel. Following the concrete walkways, these rusted surfaces are an effective complement to the lush woodlands and other planted environments that visitors can enjoy as they stroll the gardens and take in panoramic views of Barcelona.

# 2000 LA GRANJA ESCALATORS

## José Antonio Martínez Lapeña, Elías Torres Tur ▸ Toledo, Spain

Seen from the open space at the base near Paseo Recaredo, the escalators ascend in a jagged line that recalls the shape of the medieval wall below it.

Many cities in Europe have had to contend with the literal and metaphorical collision of automobiles and tourists in historic cores. The historic city of Toledo, Spain, was made a UNESCO Heritage Site in 1986, and about ten years later it embarked upon remedying its vehicular problem. As part of a larger plan by urban planner Joan Busquets to revitalize its center, the decision was made to build a four-hundred-car underground parking garage just outside the city's medieval walls and connect it to the old city 118 feet (36 meters) above by a series of escalators carved into the hillside.

The escalators, which deliver people from Paseo Recaredo at the bottom to Subida Granja at the top (hence the name), were designed by Barcelona-based architects José Antonio Martínez Lapeña (1941–) and Elías Torres Tur (1944–). Before tackling this project the duo had carried out renovations and interventions in other historic cities in Spain. In Toledo their work was as much archaeology as architecture—and as much architecture as landscape design. Archaeologically, the siting and excavation of the project's elements had to take into account historical remains so as not to damage them; a portal near the base of the escalators appears to cut into the medieval wall, yet in fact it does so below the fortified wall in order to preserve it. Architecturally, they designed the escalators to ascend the Rodadero hillside in six sections, so as to adapt to the terrain and, perhaps, in a nod to the segments of the medieval wall that they look out on. Concrete footings and retaining walls against the hillside fold over to form a cantilevered roof that covers people riding the escalators and frames views of the countryside. Yet the roof also enables the landscape to extend over the top, merging the escalators and hillside from above, and creating the distinctive jagged curve from below.

Used by tourists as well as residents who live below but work in the city center above, the escalators are an extremely popular addition to the city. They are echoed in the nearby El Greco Congress Center, which was designed by architect Rafael Moneo with its own parking garage and set of escalators encased in the hillside. In that recent project the vertical infrastructure is barely visible, unlike at La Granja, where it is celebrated as a fusion of new and old, of architecture and landscape.

# 2001 LANDSCHAFTSPARK DUISBURG-NORD

## Latz + Partner ▸ Duisburg, Germany

While much of the old Meiderich Ironworks structures are filled with cultural, entertainment, and recreational uses, the landscape around them supports walking and other idyllic pastimes.

Situated in a large green belt area in Germany's Emschler region, Landschaftspark Duisburg-Nord is an integral part of the country's Industrial Heritage Trail, which links formerly industrial areas in the Ruhr River basin. Latz + Partner's 1990 competition-winning design quickly became a popular precedent for regenerating obsolete industrial lands for good reason: instead of creating a tabula rasa surface for development, it celebrates the area's past by integrating industrial fragments with the new landscapes. Parts of the park opened to the public in 1994, but 2001 marks the opening of the visitor center, a launch point for exploring the park.

Although the design by landscape architect Peter Latz (1939–) with his wife and business partner, Anneliese Latz (1940–), is not the first integration of landscape and industrial infrastructure—that honor goes to Richard Haag's Gas Works Park in Seattle (see 1975)—it is easily the largest, at 445 acres (180 hectares). Unlike Haag's creation, whose industrial structures were eventually fenced off due to safety concerns, Landschaftspark Duisburg-Nord significantly incorporates the relics of the century-old, former Meiderich Ironworks into the use of the park: people move through the blast furnaces on new walkways; the gasometer, now clean, is home to a scuba diving class; the blower house, casting house, and power plant host concerts, films, and other events; the railroad tracks serve as bike paths; and playgrounds are cut into old ore bunkers. Nearly everything has been reused in some manner.

With its pathways, waterways, and gardens inserted into the ruined landscape, Latz's design strikes a remarkable balance between designed and found, formal and informal; in effect it creates a strange hybrid in the process. Something as practical, and to many people as ugly, as an industrial complex has been preserved as part of Germany's cultural heritage and transformed into a place of enjoyment. The amusement is particularly pronounced at night, when a light installation by the British artist Jonathan Park bathes the rust-red structures in all the colors of the rainbow.

# 2002 MFO-PARK

## Burckhardt+Partner, Raderschall Partner ▸ Zürich, Switzerland

From the outside, MFO-Park looks like a building covered in climbing plants that part at the base to provide access.

Seating is provided inside the park at ground level as well as at lookouts accessed by a network of stairs between the green walls.

What makes an urban park? In too many instances the land is treated as a sort of green oasis in the hardscape of the city, with trees, lawns, and flowers contrasting with the built surroundings. In other instances the opposite is the case, and hard surfaces outnumber soft ones, making these spaces more plazas than parks. MFO-Park in Zürich's Oerlikon district straddles these two situations through something unmistakably urban: verticality.

MFO-Park takes its name from the former Maschinenfabrik Oerlikon, the factory that occupied the site for about a hundred years. It and other area factories closed in the late 1990s, paving the way for Neu-Oerlikon, a master plan with office buildings, residences, shopping centers, and cultural components. The plan included four distinctive parks, with MFO-Park occupying a full 2-acre (.8-hectare) block near the Zürich Oerlikon train station. In a truly multidisciplinary design, the architectural firm Burckhardt+Partner and landscape architecture firm Raderschall Partner together won a 1998 competition with what they called a "Park House" concept.

Three sides of the 111 foot (34 meters) wide by 328 foot (100 meters) long site are bound by a double-walled steel frame measuring 60 feet (18 meters) tall covered in a gridded wire mesh, which is an armature for over twelve hundred thousand climbing plants. One end of the short side is kept open to invite people into the central space, which feels like a large hall thanks to the open, steel-frame roof. Benches, pools, and blue-green glass pebbles define a smaller space on the ground level, where the tapered bases of the steel framing draw the eye upward. Stairs draw people physically upward into the three-story structure where they can lounge on a sundeck at the very top, look down on the central space from cantilevered lookouts, or, through signage, learn about some of the one hundred plant species used in the park.

Since the park's inauguration in 2002, the plants have grown to cover the sides of the "largest pergola in the world" (much larger than the ones in the nearby Gustav-Ammann-Park—see 1942) remarkably well, thanks in part to a complex system of water collection and irrigation, and the thoughtful selection of plants. Depending on the time of year one visits, the vegetal "walls" are sparse, full, or colorful. At night, the "Park House" turns into a public theater, when neon lights and spotlights bathe the structure and its green cover in a colorful glow.

# 2003 PARQUE DA JUVENTUDE

## aflalo / gasperini, Rosa Kliass ▸ São Paulo, Brazil

Visitors can ascend new walkways to stroll atop the concrete ruin of the former prison wall, here parallel to Carajás Creek.

The skate park and playing fields on the eastern portion of the site sit next to a women's prison that is still in operation.

The contributions of landscape architects in Brazil—in fact, all of South America—have a way of being overshadowed by Roberto Burle Marx, the prolific and one-of-a-kind designer of thousands of landscapes last century (see 1949 and 1950). Women landscape architects, by virtue of underrepresentation in the profession, have an even larger hurdle to overcome. Rosa Kliass (1932–) is a Brazilian landscape architect whose name deserves to be known as widely as Burle Marx's; Parque da Juventude (Youth Park) in São Paulo is an important later work in her long career.

Like many landscape architects, Kliass started in private practice designing residential gardens, but after meeting architect Jorge Wilheim she shifted to public sector work with an emphasis on urban and environmental issues. She worked on projects with Wilheim as well as on Jaime Lerner's ambitious plan for Curitiba and park projects in São Paulo. For Parque da Juventude, located on the site of the once-notorious Carandiru Penitentiary, Kliass was part of a team led by the architecture firm aflalo/gasperini. They won a competition in 1999 to turn a place of tragedy (most notably the 1992 Carandiru massacre) into a community space with a park, institutional buildings, and recreational facilities.

The 60-acre (24-hectare) site's irregular shape allowed the park to be organized and realized in three phases, with the first opening in 2003 and the whole done by 2006. On the east is the sports park with its skateboard park and basketball and tennis courts. The west area consists of open spaces and cultural facilities, such as a public library, that are just steps from the Carandiru subway station. In the center is the park's most unique landscape, where Kliass and the other designers confronted the history of the site directly: salvaged walls of the prison are turned into walkways that the public can traverse, intertwined with new walkways made from COR-TEN steel framing. This section of the well-trafficked park is notable for its dramatic ruins and elevated walk through the dense trees, but the Parque da Juventude is also important for its environmental restoration of Carajás Creek, which bisects the site, and for providing a public space for an underprivileged population in Brazil's largest metropolis.

# 2004 MILLENNIUM PARK

## Skidmore, Owings & Merrill ▸ Chicago, Illinois, United States

The Michigan Avenue street wall overlooks Millennium Park on the west, while on the east Frank Gehry's curling bridge connects to Maggie Daley Park, formerly Daley Bicentennial Plaza.

Gehry's band shell and trellis are visible over the "shoulder hedge" of the Lurie Garden, which Kathryn Gustafson designed as a miniature of Chicago's *Urbs in horto* (City in a Garden) motto.

At the turn of the twenty-first century, Chicago took a half-billion-dollar gamble on turning a former rail yard and parking lot on prime land into a park that would draw visitors from all over the world. Although hardly the most ambitious plan for the city that reversed the flow of its river a century before, the park notably combined innovative architecture, sculptures, and landscape designs into a hard-to-ignore package. Millennium Park's success since opening in July 2004 relies heavily on these disparate pieces.

Chicago was faced with the need to deck over the equivalent of six city blocks because in the mid-1800s it gave a right-of-way east of Michigan Avenue to a railroad in exchange for building a breakwater. In those days Lake Michigan extended to the namesake avenue, but after the Great Fire of 1871 portions were filled in to create Grant Park. The northernmost sections remained open wounds in the cityscape until 1977, when Richard J. Daley Bicentennial Plaza (named for the six-term mayor) was built above a parking garage a couple of blocks east of Michigan Avenue. That park served as a precedent for the neighboring Millennium Park, but it took another twenty years for a successful plan to emerge. Daley's son, Richard M. Daley, in the third of his own six terms as mayor, hired Chicago's go-to architecture and planning firm Skidmore, Owings & Merrill (SOM) to develop a master plan that placed a 17-acre (6.9-hectare) park atop a 2,126-car parking garage that would bridge over the remaining tracks still in operation.

The park's western half near historic Michigan Avenue, with landscape architecture by Terry Guen Design Associates, maintained SOM's neoclassical design: walkways on axis with the Loop's east-west streets, a re-created neoclassical peristyle, and a restaurant in a low limestone building. But the specially commissioned artworks on this half are not so sedate: Anish Kapoor's bean-shaped *Cloud Gate* reflects a distorted skyline and Jaume Plensa's *Crown Fountain* splashes people with water spewed from digital faces on glass-block towers. The architectural contributions on the eastern half depart from the neoclassical master plan, most notably Frank Gehry's billowing band shell with its trellis arching over an elliptical lawn and Kathryn Gustafson's Lurie Garden with Piet Oudolf's perennial plantings. Although these four main attractions do little to relate to one another or create a cohesive whole, they congeal into a tourist magnet that residents can enjoy, too.

# 2005 CHEONGGYECHEON RIVER PARK

## SeoAhn Total Landscape ▸ Seoul, South Korea

Seen from a pedestrian bridge near its western terminus, the sunken Cheonggyecheon River Park reintroduced the watercourse that a double-decker highway covered for more than thirty years.

One outcome of progress and modernization in the last century was the insertion of highways—many of them elevated—into urban areas all over the world. Over time some cities looked for alternatives from the increased traffic, noise, and pollution they brought. Boston spent over $15 billion on its high-profile "Big Dig," and Madrid spent $5 billion to bury the M-30 along the Manzanares River (see 2011). The even more daring (and cheaper, at less than $1 billion) Cheonggyecheon River Park in Seoul completely removed an elevated highway and replaced it with a public space.

Suffering from flooding and pollution in Seoul's early days, the Cheonggyecheon became a drainage channel in the 1400s and over time saw development by an economically and politically marginalized population along its edges. Given this last fact, the stream was considered a suitable site for a highway serving central Seoul, first as a surface road capping the waterway and then as a second level raised on concrete pylons and completed in 1970. A fact of life for younger residents, it was a scar to be removed for Myung-bak Lee in his successful bid for mayor of Seoul in 2002. In only twenty-seven months he was able to move through the demolition of the 3.5-mile (5.6-kilometer) highway, the installation of underground infrastructure, and the construction of public spaces along the unearthed river, plus the beefing up of public transit in the city to offset the loss of driving lanes.

Completed in October 2005, Cheonggyecheon River Park starts on the west at an at-grade plaza and a fountain with steps down to the walkways next to the water, about 24 feet (7.3 meters) below the level of the streets above. The stream terminates on the east in a 280-acre (113-hectare) forest preserve. Overseen by SeoAhn Total Landscape, the park goes under twenty-seven crossings, many of them new pedestrian bridges, is punctuated by spaces designed by other landscape architects (Boston's Mikyoung Kim designed the sunken stone garden near the western entrance), and features two historical relics: a pair of the highway's concrete pylons and rebuilt storefronts that echo what used to line the stream's edges. More than a pleasant stroll in the middle of Seoul, the park can boast of less air pollution, a lower ambient temperature, increased biodiversity, and economic returns that would make any city consider doing away with its elevated highways.

# 2006 AUSTRALIAN GARDEN, ROYAL BOTANIC GARDENS

**Taylor Cullity Lethlean** ▸ **Cranbourne, Australia**

The influence of painter Fred Williams's abstract canvases on Taylor Cullity Lethlean is apparent in this aerial view of the Red Sand Garden in the foreground and the "river bend" beyond.

Positioned alongside the Red Sand Garden, Greg Clarke's long COR-TEN steel sculpture borders a water feature that leads visitors toward the rest of the garden.

A garden that attempts to portray a whole country will no doubt consist of some abstraction, especially when that country is Australia—an island so large it's a continent. The Australian Garden, covering 61 acres (25 hectares) at the Royal Botanic Gardens in Cranbourne, near Melbourne, displays the country's flora in a manner that is artistic, while at the same time serving as a place of education and inspiration.

Taylor Cullity Lethlean (T.C.L.), the firm of Kevin Taylor (1953–2012), Kate Cullity (1956–), and Perry Lethlean (1956–), won the competition for the Australian Garden in 1995, when political debates—a.k.a. "The History Wars"—were contending with the country's history and national identity. Like other landscape architects at the time, T.C.L. moved beyond the prevailing "Sydney Bush School" designs, which balanced modernist aesthetics with ecological awareness, toward a more playful and sculptural approach integrating native and indigenous plants. Asked in the competition brief to explore the role of native flora in shaping Australia, display native flora in creative ways, and celebrate plants in Australian culture, T.C.L. responded with bold forms painted across the surface of the botanical garden. The first stage, which abstracted the island's sandy interior, was completed in 2006 and the second stage, moving to Australia's coastlines, was done in 2012; both were done with planting designer Paul Thompson.

Within the larger Australian Garden are nearly thirty smaller gardens and areas, ranging from the expansive Red Sand Garden to the Rockpool Waterway and the aptly named Weird & Wonderful Garden. Visitors confront the Red Sand Garden after moving through the visitor center; here, red sand is dotted with native plants and, in the foreground, an installation by artists Edwina Kearney and Mark Stoner that utilizes ceramic pieces to depict water in Australia's arid interior. Other contributions by artists and architects are found throughout the Australian Garden, including a massive COR-TEN steel sculpture by Greg Clarke and toilet shelters by BKK Architects. Between the sandy first stage and watery second stage is Gibson Hill, a prime spot for taking in views of the Red Sand Garden and Rockpool Waterway. Or to put it another way, here is where the two parts of Australia's abstracted landscape come together into one.

# 2007 OLYMPIC SCULPTURE PARK

**Weiss/Manfredi** ▸ **Seattle, Washington, United States**

The shift in the United States in the late twentieth century from manufacturing and other blue-collar industries to the white-collar, service sector meant cities had numerous opportunities for development in their formerly industrial waterfronts—ideal if only for the fact that these areas were often cut off from the cities beyond by railroads and highways. Seattle's Olympic Sculpture Park is an excellent case in point, one in which architecture and landscape overcame the obstacles of the industrial and highway ages.

Looking back to the nineteenth century, the site of the Seattle Art Museum's (SAM) Olympic Sculpture Park north of downtown was characterized by the steep bluff of Denny Hill, which was leveled at the turn of the century for industrial development. A petroleum transfer and distribution facility occupied the three-block site from 1910 until 1999, when SAM, with the Trust for Public Land, purchased the three-parcel property. Two years later the New York firm of husband-and-wife architects Marion Weiss (1957–) and Michael Manfredi (1953–) won a design competition for the 8.5-acre (3.4-hectare) sculpture park with a cross-disciplinary approach that resulted in a project more landscape than building—a promenade that merges landscape and infrastructure much like Seattle's own Freeway Park (see 1976).

The sculpture park zigzags from a high point of 40 feet (12 meters) above the water's edge, where a glass pavilion is located, and bridges four lanes of traffic and a freight line to end in a restored beach on the edge of Elliott Bay. The 2,200-foot (670-meter) path—what Weiss and Manfredi describe as a landform and is shaped like a "Z" when seen from overhead—is made up of a number of micro-settings with artworks and native plantings, most significantly Richard Serra's *Wake* at the base of the pavilion's amphitheater, Alexander Calder's bright-red *Eagle*, Teresita Fernández's glass *Seattle Cloud Cover* mural over the BNSF rail line, and Mark Dion's *Neukom Vivarium*. The last echoes the cross-disciplinary approach of Weiss/Manfredi: part art, architecture, and landscape, the piece consists of a 60-foot-long (18-meter) "nurse log" removed from the forest and housed in a greenhouse designed in collaboration with the architects. It and the other artworks give people a reason to venture to the Olympic Sculpture Park, but it's the city and its surroundings that are put on display, as each turn of the promenade highlights different parts of the skyline, the bay, and the infrastructure it traverses.

The Z-shaped sculpture park descends from the glass pavilion on the left to a beach along Elliott Bay, crossing Elliott Avenue and a freight line in the process.

# 2008 QINHUANGDAO RED RIBBON PARK

**Turenscape** ▸ **Qinhuangdao, China**

The red ribbon stands out as an artificial line in the green landscape, though strategically placed holes in the 2-foot-high (20-centimeter) bench allow plant species to grow through its surface.

China's rampant urbanization in the twenty-first century has been accompanied by a widespread destruction of the country's landscape and related environmental problems: air pollution, a lack of clean water, and a scarcity of food from the loss of agricultural land. After attending the Harvard University Graduate School of Design, landscape architect Kongjian Yu (1963–) returned to his native China in 1997 determined to pave an alternative path. His ambitions were met with resistance from other landscape architects and planners, but through efforts aimed directly at politicians of the highest order, Yu's firm, Turenscape, has managed to create some of the most exciting and ecologically advanced landscape designs in China—or anywhere, for that matter.

One year after his return to China, Yu set up Turenscape and five years later established what is now the College of Architecture and Landscape Architecture at Peking University. The school carries out research on ecological infrastructure at regional and even national scales—an extension of Yu's thesis at Harvard—and his firm extends this research into the field. One of the most exciting outcomes of the research is the development of so-called sponge cities, where landscapes (not actually whole cities) are designed to clean water and remediate contaminated soil, all the while serving as beautiful places for people to enjoy. Some of Turenscape's most striking work in the realm of sponge cities has been carried out in Qinhuangdao, a port city in China's northern Hebei province. Two of the four projects built there to date are linked by a bridge crossing the Tanghe River: Qinhuangdao Botanic Garden and Qinhuangdao Red Ribbon Park.

Completed in 2008, one year before the botanical garden, the 50-acre (20-hectare) Red Ribbon Park is an apt moniker: a bright-red, fiber-steel bench with built-in lighting snakes for 1,640 feet (500 meters) through the linear park on the river's east bank. This feature splits the park into two halves: dense trees, pavilions, and the occasional formal garden on the east, and the natural river corridor on the west. The red ribbon and adjacent boardwalk invite visitors to walk its length and learn about the river habitat that has been preserved through the introduction of this element. Reportedly costing less than Turenscape's fee on the project, the red ribbon is a simple and inexpensive means of creating environmental infrastructure and an eye-catching alternative to intensive and costly ornamental gardens that have accompanied China's massive urbanization.

# 2009 ORPHEUS AT BOUGHTON

## Kim Wilkie ▸ Kettering, England

A solitary figure in the lower-right corner of the inverted pyramid's basin gives a sense of scale to the large landform that mirrors the older truncated pyramid across the canal.

Remote-controlled bank mowers keep the angled grass walls of the old and new landforms crisp.

Although Land art, in the guise of creations like Robert Smithson's *Spiral Jetty* (see 1970), is a twentieth-century creation, landforms—the manipulation of large swaths of land for symbolic effect—date back centuries. Although not purely a British phenomenon, the British Isles have a great history of landforms, stemming from durable soils and grasses, steady rain, and low light that accentuates the shaped landscapes. Designer Kim Wilkie's (1956–) infatuation with landforms has led him to create contemporary interpretations, none more lyrical than Orpheus at Boughton House in England's East Midlands.

The present Boughton House dates back to the late 1600s, when Ralph Montagu, the first Duke of Montagu, inherited the house and its 11,000 acres (4,450 hectares). Following his death, his son John modeled the landscape adjacent to the house on Versailles, earning the place the moniker "The English Versailles." As one of the few survivors of the eighteenth-century transition from formal French baroque to picturesque English parkland, the estate is historically important and a protected landmark that happens to have its own landform: Charles Bridgeman's truncated grass pyramid from 1724, built to serve as the base for a mausoleum that was never realized.

Next to the mount and the right-angled, canalized River Ise is the site Wilkie was given in 2004 by the Duke of Buccleuch, the house's current owner, as he restored the gardens. After determining the site was free of archaeological remains, Wilkie proposed an inverted pyramid—an Orpheus Hades to complement the Olympian Mount, inspired by the myth in which Orpheus voyages to the underworld to save his wife, Eurydice. Cut into the earth with angled grass walls at the same angle as the mount, Orpheus at Boughton features a gentle ramp that allows visitors to descend to the pool of water 23 feet (7 meters) below the surrounding landscape. Adjacent to the inverted pyramid is an extension with a golden section rectangle; its Renaissance- and Bridgeman-inspired geometries are marked with grass paths and a spiral rill of water that culminates in a steel-framed cube. Myth and geometry fuse at Orpheus at Boughton in a landscape that allows one to simultaneously peer at the reflected sky and into the hidden underworld below.

# 2010 MOSES BRIDGE

## RO&AD Architecten ▸ Halsteren, Netherlands

The line that Moses Bridge cuts through the moat and embankments maintains the view of Fort de Roovere that invading armies would have found centuries ago.

Only one glance is needed to see why this bridge in the province of Noord Brabant in southwestern Holland has taken on the name Moses Bridge: the walls of the bridge seem to part the water to provide access *through* a moat rather than *over* it, as is typical with most bridges. The name makes it seem that the bridge is a one-liner, albeit a clever one, but the design by Dutch architects RO&AD (Ro Koster [1963–] and Ad Kil [1965–]) is rooted strongly in the area's military history as well as its recreational and cultural transformations this century.

Moses Bridge provides access to the earthwork Fort de Roovere, which dates to 1628 and the country's West Brabant Water Line. In this defense system, parts of the low-lying country were flooded to stop invading armies, particularly Spain during the Eighty Years' War. The military fortifications fell into disrepair in the nineteenth century, when new technologies made the water line obsolete. This century Noord Brabant has been carrying out the West Brabant Water Line project, which consists of nine subprojects. One of them, Moses Bridge, was realized in 2010 by RO&AD Architecten, who felt that a more traditional bridge would mar the purity of the historical artifact. RO&AD have been responsible for a few other distinctive subprojects: the floating Ravelijn Bridge, which provides access to a 1702 island fortress in Bergen op Zoom; Bunkertreppe, a wooden stair that offers a lookout over a concrete World War II bunker in De Heen; and Pompejus, a watchtower and performance venue that started construction near Fort de Roovere in 2016. Of these, Moses Bridge is as much of a draw as is the attraction it provides access to.

Even before walking between the water, visitors approaching from the east—the direction of invaders centuries ago—are embraced by two chest-high walls that cut through the embankments, as they do on the fort side. Steps lead down to the bridge, which is formed by wood sheet pilings on the side and hardwood decking underfoot. Water stops right at the top of the wood walls, a level maintained by adjustable outflow dams. Although it involved some complex engineering and construction to pull off, the design is simple, an unexpected, why-didn't-I-think-of-that synthesis of Holland's distinctive natural and historical circumstances in miniature.

# 2011 MADRID RÍO

## MRIO Arquitectos, West 8 ▸ Madrid, Spain

The six-lane Avenida de Portugal was buried in a tunnel below a parking garage and park; it meets the Madrid Río at Esplanade del Rey, with its flowery paving patterns.

Now a pedestrian path planted with trees, the diagonal line crossing the Manzanares River follows the path the M-30 beltway once took aboveground.

An obvious fact: automobiles and pedestrians don't mix; high-speed movement and safe public spaces can't exist in one place. In the case of the huge Madrid Río project, a highway buried in a tunnel and an aboveground park are two sides of the same coin: one does not exist without the other. Unlike most cities that circled their downtowns with highways in the middle of the last century, Madrid Río undid its beltway, the M-30, which was completed in 1974 but obsolete thirty years later.

As would be expected in an infrastructural project more than 6 miles (10 kilometers) long, politics played an important role. Mayor Alberto Ruiz-Gallardón Jiménez's two terms (2003–11) enabled the tunneling of 34 miles (56 kilometers) of the M-30 and the creation of the Madrid Río project along the Manzanares River southwest of the city center (the highway tunnel was built during his first term and Madrid Río was realized during his second term). A two-stage competition for the design and development of the public spaces was held in 2005, and a trio of Spanish architecture offices under the name MRIO Arquitectos (Burgos & Garrido, Porras La Casta, and Rubio & Álvarez-Sala) with Dutch landscape architecture firm West 8 beat out the other seven finalists. Their proposal looked at the larger context of the Manzanares—from the mountains in the north to the Jarama River in the south—and envisioned the section threading through the city as a "necklace of vegetable pearls": a riverfront promenade connecting the dozens of smaller projects (parks, playgrounds, fountains, sports facilities, buildings, pedestrian bridges) that make up the larger Madrid Río project.

Construction of the tunnel involved the draining of the river and the temporary rerouting of six lanes of traffic, so by the time Madrid Río opened to the public in April 2011 it was considered "the wound that healed." The realization of a green park living over the tunnels involved the planting of 33,500 trees and 460,000 shrubs across its seven main landscapes. Of these, the Salón de Pinos is the largest, extending along the river's right bank to link the project's new urban spaces, while the Avenida de Portugal perpendicular to the river is a neighborhood park atop a buried roadway and parking garage for one thousand cars. Parkland sits above, but the ramps to the parking garage remind people that the undertaking is essentially a massive piece of infrastructure.

# 2012 BAY SOUTH, GARDENS BY THE BAY

## Grant Associates ▸ Singapore

Singapore is home this century to some of the largest and most eye-catching buildings, going hand in hand with the island city-state's density and enormous wealth. Most notable is Marina Bay Sands, a resort and convention center complex designed by architect Moshe Safdie as three sloping slabs connected at top by a Sky Park with pool, restaurant, and cantilevered observation deck. But over-the-top design statements in Singapore aren't limited to buildings, as the adjacent Gardens by the Bay attests.

Both Marina Bay Sands and Gardens by the Bay are located on nearly 900 acres (360 hectares) of reclaimed land east of the Downtown Core and separated from it by Marina Bay. Prime Minister Lee Hsien Loong confidently announced the Gardens by the Bay project in 2005 as a future national icon. With a total area of 250 acres (101 hectares), the gardens were divided into three precincts: Bay East, Bay Central, and Bay South. A team led by UK landscape architecture firm Grant Associates won a 2006 competition for the master plan of Bay South, which opened in June 2012 on 133 acres (54 hectares) immediately south of Marina Bay Sands. Although inspired by the organization and physiology of the orchid, Singapore's national flower, the designers developed a plan that is reliant ultimately upon complex engineering, intelligent environmental infrastructure, and attention-getting architecture.

As built, Bay South is made up of theme gardens, cultural gardens, a children's garden, and a lake, but it is anchored by two hard-to-miss features: the Cooled Conservatories and the Supertrees. Designed by London architects Wilkinson Eyre, the conservatories house 226,000 plants, with the Flower Dome replicating a cool, dry Mediterranean climate, and the Cloud Forest bringing vegetation from cool, moist Tropical Montane regions to flat, humid Singapore. The eighteen Supertrees, designed by Grant Associates, range in height from 82 to 164 feet (25 to 50 meters) and feature an elevated walkway, more than 150,000 plants climbing their "trunks," and a rooftop bar at the top of the tallest. Further, two of the Supertrees tie into the garden's environmental infrastructure: one exhausts the heat extracted from the conservatories and one releases gases from the biomass boilers used to generate power. With these multifaceted roles, the striking Supertrees are suitably at home among Singapore's iconic buildings.

Although walking the grounds of Bay South is free, access to the OCBC Skyway, raised 72 feet (22 meters) in the air, requires an admission fee.

# 2013 PARCO PORTELLO

## Charles Jencks, Andreas Kipar ▸ Milan, Italy

The Parco Portello and its adjacent developments are connected to their surroundings in this section of Milan through pedestrian bridges.

One of the strongest proponents—if not the only—for discovering and embedding cosmological meaning in landforms is Charles Jencks (1939–), the influential author and architecture critic who also has designed a number of landscapes in the United Kingdom and beyond. In the early 1990s, around the time he wrote *The Architecture of the Jumping Universe*, which advocated for architects to embrace chaos theory, complexity, and morphogenesis, Jencks started the Garden of Cosmic Speculation on his own 30 acres (12 hectares) in Dumfries, Scotland. While that is his most famous cosmological landscape design, the Parco Portello (Spirals of Time) in Milan is his most public creation.

In 2002 Jencks was hired by shopping-mall magnate Marco Brunelli to design a 17-acre (6.8-hectare) park on a portion of land that formerly served as the Alfa Romeo Portello Plant. Originally on the outskirts northwest of Milan, the Portello area was engulfed by the city over time and now finds itself home to the Milano Congressi (the largest convention center in Europe), as well as new office, residential, and retail developments. Working with landscape architect Andreas Kipar (1960–) of Milan's LAND Group on the decade-plus design and realization, Jencks defined the park as three mounds, with the tallest spiraling up 75 feet (22.8 meters) as if to cut off the rest of the park from its surroundings but also make it known among the district's mid-rise buildings.

The theme of the park—Spirals of Time—is expressed through the mounds, each representing a period of cultural time in Milan: Prehistory, History, and Present. The entrance up a flight of stairs from the road on the south brings visitors to the Present mound (the tallest), whose spiraling path culminates in a sculpture of a DNA helix. The Prehistory mound curls like the formation of a galaxy, wrapping around a circular pond near the park's center, while the arcing History mound shields the children's playground near the north edge of the park. On the north is also where the Time Garden is found: a straight path where circular plantings and intricate paving patterns intersect to mark the cycles of time, from one rotation of the earth to the universe's 13.7 billion years of existence. Deciphering the symbolism Jencks inserted throughout is hardly intuitive, but it's not a prerequisite to enjoying the park.

# 2014 THE HIGH LINE

## James Corner Field Operations, Diller Scofidio + Renfro, Piet Oudolf
## New York City, United States

A glass guardrail at the southern tip of the High Line cuts a section through the layers of the park and reused industrial infrastructure.

The only patch of lawn on the whole High Line, found between 22nd and 23rd Streets, is (when open) a popular spot for lounging.

This 1.5-mile (2.4-kilometer) elevated park built atop a derelict railroad on Manhattan's West Side is easily the most influential piece of landscape architecture of the twenty-first century. The Sydney suburb of Ultimo was the first to follow suit with the Goods Line built atop an old railway corridor, but numerous cities around the world have been eyeing outdated infrastructure to reap benefits like New York's—over $2 billion in residential and commercial development per some estimates.

Manhattan's elevated railroad was built in 1934 after more than a half century of conflicts between pedestrians and freight cars running at grade up and down "Death Avenue" near the Hudson River waterfront. Although heralded as a marvel at the time for the way it skirted the streets and actually ran through buildings, the elevated line functioned at capacity until only 1960, with sections demolished as late as 1991. A community meeting in 1999 found that most of the people in attendance wanted the rest to come down. Two strangers who wanted to save it, Joshua David and Robert Hammond, fortuitously sat next to each other at the meeting and soon after started Friends of the High Line. They drummed up enough support and funds for preservation to gain city approval and to hold a design competition for the future park.

The team led by the landscape architecture firm of James Corner (1961–) with the architecture firm Diller Scofidio + Renfro and planting designer Piet Oudolf (1944–) won the competition with a design that aimed to capture the interim landscape of plants and wildflowers that had taken over in the previous decades. A system of precast concrete planks that taper to finger with native plantings runs throughout, interspersed with special episodes, such as a sunken amphitheater over Tenth Avenue, a flyover through a canopy of trees, and a playground where kids can crawl between the structure's steel beams.

Construction began on the first section, from Gansevoort Street on the south to 20th Street on the north, in 2006 and opened in 2009 to great acclaim. It was not until the opening of the third section in 2014, though, that the whole length of the High Line (up to 34th Street) could be traversed. Construction of high-profile apartment and office buildings is culminating in the massive Hudson Yards development, which would be a different beast entirely without this elevated park wrapping around it.

# 2015 GRANDE CRETTO

## Alberto Burri ▸ Gibellina, Sicily, Italy

Some of the most prominent pieces of Land art are ambitious works that take decades to complete. These include Michael Heizer's *City*, which he started in Nevada in 1972 and is slated to open in 2020; Charles Ross's monumental *Star Axis* in New Mexico, which he started building in 1976 and is nearing completion; and James Turrell's *Roden Crater* project in New Mexico, which the artist has been adding his "skyspaces" to since buying an extinct volcano in 1979. The *Grande Cretto* by Italian artist Alberto Burri (1915–1995) is in Europe but at home on this list; conceived in 1981 and partially completed in 1989, the 40-acre (16-hectare) sculpture was completed in 2015, twenty years after the artist's death and the hundredth anniversary of his birth.

The artwork takes its name from Burri's *Cretto* paintings, which he first displayed in 1973 and made him famous worldwide. Typically made from acrylic and polyvinyl alcohol on cellotex, the minimalist canvases featured cracks (*cretto* is "crack" in Italian) or fissures that formed from the accumulation of materials and their process of drying over time. When invited by Mayor Ludovico Corrao in the early 1980s to contribute an artwork to Gibellina Nuova, the replacement for the Sicilian town destroyed in a 1968 earthquake, Burri refused and instead proposed a giant white concrete *Cretto* over the remains of the old town. Located about 11 miles (18 kilometers) to the east of the new town, *Grande Cretto*'s fissures reference the streets of the old town while also expressing the seismic destruction of the magnitude 6.4 earthquake that killed about one thousand people and left around one hundred thousand homeless in Gibellina and the surrounding towns.

The winding thirty-minute drive from Gibellina Nuova to *Grande Cretto* takes visitors past the old town's cemetery—its irregular grid and tree-lined path are echoed in the layout of the artwork and the weeds that have grown in the 1989 section. The new section, which comes close to touching the roadway, is bright white compared to the old section. But a more revealing contrast is found in the ruined remains of the town that were not compacted and used as fill for Burri's sculpture; these buildings, south of the completed sculpture, speak of the enormous loss that affected the small town all those decades ago. Burri's powerful statement takes on added meaning through the preservation of these ruins.

# 2016 THE PARK

## !melk ▸ Las Vegas, Nevada, United States

The west end of the Park, away from the strip, is anchored by artist Marco Cochrane's sculpture *Bliss Dance*, which first appeared at Burning Man in Nevada's Black Rock Desert.

The rust-red shade structures that reach up to 60 feet (18 meters) were made by a shipbuilding company in the Netherlands and shipped to Las Vegas in sections for assembly.

Lined with casinos, malls, and hotels that depend on air-conditioning to provide their guests a respite from the desert heat, the Las Vegas strip seems like an unlikely place to find a new park. But cities this century are well aware of the potential of urban landscapes, particularly in regard to spurring development and increasing the value of adjacent real estate—consider it the High Line effect (see 2014). With the Park, as it's simply called, MGM Resorts International hopes to carry this phenomenon to the city in the desert with the first-ever park on the strip.

Vegas is a much different beast today than it was in its early years, or even when Denise Scott Brown and Robert Venturi famously studied it in the late 1960s. Sure, the automobile still reigns, but only a few large companies run the casinos and resorts, which are connected to one another by a network of walkways, escalators, and pedestrian bridges that span the strip and adjacent thoroughfares. In a sense this network, which gets people outside, has primed visitors for a full-blown park. The Park is located on a narrow 6-acre (2.4-hectare) site along a reconfigured Park Avenue, perpendicular to the strip and between two of MGM's fourteen Vegas properties—Monte Carlo and New York-New York—and adjacent to the new T-Mobile Arena. The Park serves as an entrance to MGM's properties as well as a venue for outdoor dining and a place to sit in the shade.

MGM hired two New York firms (Cooper Robertson and !melk) to master plan and lead the landscape design, respectively. For !melk, founded by Jerry van Eyck (1966–) in 2010, it was important to make the Park authentic to its context, both culturally and naturally. Therefore the design features large-scale steel shade sculptures illuminated at night, a nod to the strip's iconic architecture, and plants and trees of the Mojave region, an attempt at re-creating an oasis in the desert. This effect is heightened by the addition of head-high water walls, which create a cooling microclimate and entice people away from the strip and into the Park. Further, since MGM wanted a "finished" park from the moment it opened in April 2016, the mature trees, combined with the treelike steel sculptures, already offered a good deal of shade. With an empty lot one day and the strip's first park the next, the oasis analogy is spot-on.

# TIMELINE

**1917**   **Filoli | Bruce Porter, Isabella Worn | Woodside, California, United States**

Liliuokalani Park and Gardens / Hilo, Hawaii, United States

Rock Garden, Brooklyn Botanic Garden / New York City, United States

American City Planning Institute (later American Institute of Planners) formed.

▸ Henry Vincent Hubbard and Theodora Kimball Hubbard's *An Introduction to the Study of Landscape Design* published.

▸ Tony Garnier's *Cité Industrielle* published.

**1918**   **Villandry | Joachim Carvallo | Touraine, France**

Greatwood Gardens at Goddard / Frederick Law Olmsted, Arthur A. Shurcliff / Plainfield, Vermont, United States

Yorkship Village / Frederick Lee Ackerman / Fairview, New Jersey, United States

**1919**   **The Huntington Botanical Gardens | William Hertrich | San Marino, California, United States**

Barnsdall Art Park / Los Angeles, California, United States

Kyu Asakura House and Garden / Tokyo, Japan

Mount Assisi Gardens at the Schwab Estate / Charles Wellford Leavitt / Loretto, Pennsylvania, United States

Sonnenberg Gardens / Mary Clark Thompson, Ernest Bowditch / Canandaigua, New York, United States

**1920**   **Columbus Park | Jens Jensen | Chicago, Illinois, United States**

Kiftsgate Court Gardens / Heather Muir, Diany Binny, Anne Chambers / Chipping Campden, England

Prague Castle / Jože Plečnik / Prague, Czech Republic

▸ Welwyn Garden City founded in Hertfordshire, England.

**1921**   **Östra Kyrkogården | Sigurd Lewerentz | Malmö, Sweden**

▸ Benton MacKaye first proposed the Appalachian Trail.

**1922**   **Giardino di Ninfa | Caetani family | Sermoneta, Italy**

Country Club Plaza / J. C. Nichols / Kansas City, Missouri, United States

Mayfield Park and Preserve / Milton and Mary Mayfield Gutsch, Esteban Arredondo / Austin, Texas, United States

Morton Arboretum / Ossian Cole Simonds / Lisle, Illinois, United States

**1923**   **Jardin Majorelle | Jacques Majorelle | Marrakech, Morocco**

Stockholm Stadshuset / Ragnar Östberg / Stockholm, Sweden

**1924**   **Tuinen Mien Ruys | Mien Ruys | Dedemsvaart, Netherlands**

**1925**   **Thijsse's Hof | Jacobus Pieter Thijsse, Leonard Springer | Bloemendaal, Netherlands**

Mount Helix Nature Theater / Emerson Knight / San Diego, California, United States

▸ Exposition des Arts Décoratifs held in Paris.

▸ Le Corbusier completed his Plan Voisin for the future of Paris.

**1926**   **Naumkeag | Fletcher Steele | Stockbridge, Massachusetts, United States**

Mariebjerg Cemetery / G. N. Brandt / Gentofte, Denmark

**1927**   **Villa Noailles | Gabriel Guevrekian | Hyères, France**

Kubota Gardens / Fujitaro Kubota / Seattle, Washington, United States

**1928**   **Sunnyside Gardens | Clarence S. Stein and Henry Wright, Marjorie Sewell Cautley | New York City, United States**

Agecroft Hall / Charles Freeman Gillette / Richmond, Virginia, United States

Eaton Park / Captain Arnold Edward Sandys-Winsch / Norwich, England

▸ Congrès International d'Architecture Moderne (CIAM) founded.

**1929**   **Ladew Topiary Gardens | Harvey Smith Ladew II | Monkton, Maryland, United States**

Bok Tower Gardens / Frederick Law Olmsted Jr. / Lake Wales, Florida, United States

Cruden Farm / Edna Walling / Langwarrin, Australia

Radburn / Clarence Stein, Henry Wright, Marjorie Cautley / Radburn, New Jersey, United States

▸ The Institute of Landscape Architects (now Landscape Institute) founded in London.

▸ Le Corbusier's *The City of To-morrow and Its Planning* published.

**1930**   **Sissinghurst Castle Garden | Vita Sackville-West, Harold Nicolson | Kent, England**

Governor's Mansion / Arthur A. Shurcliff / Williamsburg, Virginia, United States

Hufeisensiedlung / Bruno Taut, Leberecht Migge / Berlin, Germany

Frogner Park / Gustav Vigeland / Oslo, Norway

**1931 Innisfree Garden | Walter Beck, Lester Collins | Millbrook, New York, United States**

Camden Library Amphitheatre / Fletcher Steele / Camden, Maine, United States

Mughal Gardens / Edwin Lutyens / New Delhi, India

▸ Jean Canneel-Claes designed a functionalist garden for his own residence in Belgium.

▸ *Regional Plan of New York and Its Environs* published.

**1932 Promenade along the Embankments and Bridges of the Ljubljanica River | Jože Plečnik | Ljubljana, Slovenia**

Savill Garden / Eric Savill / Surrey, England

Shelter over Casa Grande National Monument / Frederick Law Olmsted Jr. / Pinal County, Arizona, United States

**1933 Aarhus University | Christian Frederik Møller, Carl Theodor Sørensen | Aarhus, Denmark**

**1934 Observatorielunden | Erik Gunnar Asplund | Stockholm, Sweden**

▸ Frank Lloyd Wright unveiled his Broadacre City model in New York.

▸ Robert Moses appointed commissioner of parks.

▸ Construction of the Reichsautobahn started in Germany.

**1935 Jubilee Pool | Captain F. Latham | Penzance, England**

The Clearing / Jens Jensen / Ellison Bay, Wisconsin, United States

Roosevelt Park / Clarence Edmund "Bud" Hollied / Albuquerque, New Mexico, United States

Governor's Palace / Arthur A. Shurcliff / Williamsburg, Virginia, United States

▸ Le Corbusier's *La Ville Radieuse* published.

▸ Works Progress Administration (WPA) formed in the United States.

**1936 Millesgården | Carl Milles | Stockholm, Sweden**

Eagle Point Park / Alfred Caldwell / Dubuque, Iowa, United States

Norris Dam State Park / Tennessee Valley Authority / Rocky Top, Tennessee, United States

▸ Scenic Blue Ridge Parkway built in the Appalachian Mountains.

**1937 Amsterdamse Bos | Cornelis van Eesteren, Jacoba Mulder | Amsterdam, Netherlands**

Appalachian Trail / Benton MacKaye / United States

Greenbelt / Rexford Guy Tugwell / Greenbelt, Maryland, United States

Los Angeles Police Academy Rock Garden / Francois Scotti / Los Angeles, California, United States

▸ *Contemporary Landscape Architecture and Its Sources* exhibition held at the San Francisco Museum of Art.

**1938 Alfred Caldwell Lily Pool | Alfred Caldwell | Chicago, Illinois, United States**

Memorial Park / Constantin Brancusi / Târgu Jiu, Romania

Opus 40 / Harvey Fite / Saugerties, New York, United States

Nelson-Atkins Museum of Art / Hare & Hare / Kansas City, Missouri, United States

Beatrixpark / Jacoba Mulder / Amsterdam, Netherlands

▸ Christopher Tunnard's *Gardens in the Modern Landscape* published.

▸ International Association of Modernist Garden Architects formed.

▸ Lewis Mumford's *The Culture of Cities* published.

**1939 Tōfuku-ji Temple Hondo Garden | Mirei Shigemori | Kyoto, Japan**

Freibad Allenmoos / Max Ernst Haefeli, Werner Moser / Zürich, Switzerland

Flushing Meadows Corona Park / Gilmore D. Clarke / New York City, United States

Santa Barbara Botanic Garden / Beatrix Farrand, Lockwood de Forest Jr. / Santa Barbara, California, United States

▸ First of three-part manifesto on modern landscape design by Garrett Eckbo, Dan Kiley, and James C. Rose published in *Architectural Record*.

▸ Jens Jensen's *Siftings* published.

▸ World's Fair held on former ash dump in Flushing Meadows, Queens, New York City.

**1940 Dumbarton Oaks | Beatrix Farrand | Washington, DC, United States**

Skogskyrkogården | Erik Gunnar Asplund and Sigurd Lewerentz | Enskede, Sweden (*100 Years, 100 Buildings*)

▸ Brenda Colvin's *Land and Landscape: Evolution, Design, and Control* published.

**1941**   **Red Rocks Park and Amphitheatre | Burnham Hoyt | Morrison, Colorado, United States**

Friendship Island / Karl Foerster / Potsdam, Germany

**1942**   **Gustav-Ammann-Park | Gustav Ammann | Zürich, Switzerland**

Bayou Bend Collection and Gardens / Ruth London, Pat Fleming, Ellen Shipman / Houston, Texas, United States

Village Green / Reginald D. Johnson; Wilson, Merrill, and Alexander; Clarence Stein / Los Angeles, California, United States

**1943**   **The Parterre Garden | Gudmund Nyeland Brandt, Poul Henningsen | Copenhagen, Denmark**

Dowling Community Garden / Minneapolis, Minnesota, United States

Michael Joseph Savage Memorial Park / Tibor Donner and Anthony Bartlett / Auckland, New Zealand

Norr Mälarstrand / Holger Blom, Erik Glemme / Stockholm, Sweden

**1944**   **Ellsworth Rock Gardens | Jack Ellsworth | Kabetogama, Minnesota, United States**

Richard D. Parker Memorial Victory Gardens / Boston, Massachusetts, United States

**1945**   **Marabouparken | Hermelin & Wedborn | Sundbyberg, Sweden**

El Pedregal / Luis Barragán / Mexico City, Mexico

▸ Atomic bombs dropped in August on Japanese cities of Hiroshima and Nagasaki.

▸ UNESCO formed in London.

**1946**   **San Antonio River Walk | Robert H. H. Hugman | San Antonio, Texas, United States**

▸ The New Towns Act established in the United Kingdom.

**1947**   **Lunuganga | Geoffrey Bawa | Bentota, Sri Lanka**

Boerner Botanical Gardens / Alfred L. Boerner / Hales Corners, Wisconsin, United States

▸ Copenhagen started its green Finger Plan.

▸ *How Does Your Garden Grow?* radio show launched on BBC.

**1948**   **Nærum Allotment Gardens | Carl Theodor Sørensen | Nærum, Denmark**

Vasaparken / Erik Glemme / Stockholm, Sweden

▸ The International Federation of Landscape Architects (IFLA) founded in Cambridge, England.

▸ Thomas Church completed Donnell Garden in Sonoma, California, notable for its kidney-shaped pool.

**1949**   **Sítio Roberto Burle Marx | Roberto Burle Marx | Rio de Janeiro, Brazil**

Australian National Botanic Gardens / Lindsay Pryor / Canberra, Australia

Mausoleo delle Fosse Ardeatine / Mario Fiorentino, Giuseppe Perugini, et al. / Rome, Italy

▸ Aldo Leopold's *A Sand County Almanac* published.

▸ Ludwig Hilberseimer's *The New Regional Pattern* published.

▸ National Parks and Access to the Countryside Act made law in the United Kingdom.

**1950**   **Parque da Cidade Roberto Burle Marx | Roberto Burle Marx | São José dos Campos, Brazil**

Jac P. Thijssepark / Christiaan P. Broerse / Amstelveen, Netherlands

▸ Garrett Eckbo's *Landscapes for Living* published.

**1951**   **Brooklyn Heights Promenade | Clarke & Rapuano | New York City, United States**

Parkmerced / Thomas Church, Robert Royston / San Francisco, California, United States

▸ Brenda Colvin became first president of the Institute of Landscape Architects.

▸ The Bundesgartenschau (BUGA) garden festival first held in Germany.

▸ John Brinckerhoff Jackson's *Landscape* magazine first published.

**1952**   **Fuente de Tláloc | Diego Rivera | Mexico City, Mexico**

People's Park / Rose and Elof Pearson / Shanghai, China

Vor Frue Kirke Plaza / Carl Theodor Sørensen / Kalundborg, Denmark

▸ Thomas Church's display garden for *Sunset* magazine completed in Menlo Park, California.

**1953**   **Abby Aldrich Rockefeller Sculpture Garden | Philip Johnson | New York City, United States**

Courtyard Garden, Kishiwada Castle / Mirei Shigemori / Kishiwada, Japan

Hollin Hills / Dan Kiley / Alexandria, Virginia, United States

▸ Christopher Tunnard's *The City of Man* published.

▸ Team X formed in opposition to CIAM.

**1954**   **Peace Memorial Park | Kenzō Tange | Hiroshima, Japan**

James Rose Center / James C. Rose / Ridgewood, New Jersey, United States

**1955**   **Mellon Square | Simonds and Simonds | Pittsburgh, Pennsylvania, United States**

Aspen Institute / Herbert Bayer / Aspen, Colorado, United States

Fragrance Garden, Brooklyn Botanic Garden / Alice Ireys / New York City, United States

Kronforth Garden / Roberto Burle Marx / Rio de Janeiro, Brazil

▸ Disneyland opened in Anaheim, California.
▸ Thomas Church's *Gardens Are for People* published.

**1956 Villa Silvio Pellico | Russell Page | Turin, Italy**

Athenian Agora Excavations and Landscaping / Ralph E. Griswold / Athens, Greece

▸ Federal Aid Highway Act passed in the United States.
▸ First Urban Design Conference held at Harvard University.
▸ Garrett Eckbo created ALCOA Forecast Garden in Los Angeles.

**1957 Philopappou Hill Path | Dimitris Pikionis | Athens, Greece**

Fay Garden / Thomas Church / San Francisco, California, United States

Miller House and Garden | Dan Kiley | Columbus, Indiana, United States (*100 Years, 100 Buildings*)

Shofuso Japanese House and Garden / Junzo Yoshimura / Philadelphia, Pennsylvania, United States

**1958 UNESCO Garden of Peace | Isamu Noguchi | Paris, France**

Giardini la Mortella / Susana Walton, Russell Page / Forio, Italy

Kagawa Prefectural Government Building / Kenzō Tange / Takamatsu, Japan

Louisiana Museum of Modern Art / Ole and Edith Nørgaard, Lea Nørgaard and Vibeke Holscher / Humlebæk, Denmark

Towers of Satellite City / Luis Barragán, Mathias Goeritz / Mexico City, Mexico

▸ *The Exploding Metropolis*, edited by William H. Whyte, published.
▸ Sylvia Crowe's *The Landscape of Power* published.

**1959 Las Arboledas | Luis Barragán | Mexico City, Mexico**

Garden of the Poets / Ernst Cramer / Hannover, Germany

National Arboretum / Frederick Law Olmsted Jr., et al. / Washington, DC, United States

Pageant of Roses Garden at Rose Hills Memorial Park / Cornell, Bridgers and Troller / Whittier, California, United States

Water Gardens / Geoffrey Jellicoe / Hemel Hempstead New Town, England

▸ CIAM disbanded.

**1960 Storm King Art Center | William Rutherford | New Windsor, New York, United States**

The Beth Chatto Gardens / Beth Chatto / Essex, England

Kaiser Center Roof Garden / Theodore Osmundson / Oakland, California, United States

Lincoln Road Mall / Morris Lapidus / Miami, Florida, United States

Third Street Promenade / Charles Luckman / Santa Monica, California, United States

▸ Brasilia inaugurated as Brazil's new capital.
▸ Kevin Lynch's *The Image of the City* published.
▸ First operational GIS (Geographic Information System) developed.

**1961 Kröller-Müller Museum | Jan Tijs Pieter Bijhouwer | Otterlo, Netherlands**

Parque del Este / Roberto Burle Marx / Caracas, Venezuela

Zuihō-in Garden / Mirei Shigemori / Kyoto, Japan

▸ Construction of the Berlin Wall began.
▸ Jane Jacobs's *The Death and Life of Great American Cities* published.
▸ John Ormsbee Simonds's *Landscape Architecture: A Manual of Environmental Planning and Design* published.

**1962 Las Pozas | Edward James | Xilitla, Mexico**

Pacific Science Center Courtyard / Minoru Yamasaki / Seattle, Washington, United States

Rijksmuseum Playground / Aldo van Eyck / Amsterdam, Netherlands

St. Catherine's College / Arne Jacobsen / Oxford, England

▸ Rachel Carson's *Silent Spring* published.

**1963 Fondazione Querini Stampalia | Carlo Scarpa | Venice, Italy**

Constitution Plaza / Sasaki, Dawson & DeMay / Hartford, Connecticut, United States

Harlow Water Gardens / Pat Gibberd, Gerry Perrin / Harlow, England

Lafayette Park / Alfred Caldwell / Detroit, Michigan, United States

▸ United States government passed Clean Air Act.

**1964 John Deere World Headquarters | Sasaki Associates | Moline, Illinois, United States**

National Museum of Anthropology / Pedro Ramírez Vázquez, Jorge Campuzano, Rafael Mijares Alcérreca / Mexico City, Mexico

Northern Aviary / Cedric Price et al. / London, England

▸ Donald Appleyard, Kevin Lynch, and John Randolph Myers's *The View from the Road* published.
▸ Elizabeth Kassler's *Modern Gardens and the Landscape* published.

**1965** **The Sea Ranch | Lawrence Halprin | Sonoma County, California, United States**

Aterro do Flamengo / Roberto Burle Marx / Rio de Janeiro, Brazil

Billy Rose Art Garden / Isamu Noguchi / Jerusalem, Israel

John F. Kennedy Memorial / Geoffrey Jellicoe / Runnymede, England

Partisan Memorial Cemetery / Bogdan Bogdanović / Mostar, Bosnia and Herzegovina

▸ United States government passed Highway Beautification Act.

**1966** **Piscina das Marés | Álvaro Siza | Leça da Palmeira, Portugal**

Estates Drive Reservoir / Robert Royston / Oakland, California, United States

Little Sparta / Ian Hamilton Finlay, Sue Finlay / Dunsyre, Scotland

Lovejoy Plaza / Lawrence Halprin / Portland, Oregon, United States

▸ Australian Institute of Landscape Architects established.
▸ Ian McHarg, John O. Simonds, and four other landscape architects published "A Declaration of Concern."
▸ Landscape Architecture Foundation founded in Philadelphia.

**1967** **Paley Park | Zion & Breen | New York City, United States**

Adventure Playground / Richard Dattner / New York City, United States

Franklin D. Murphy Sculpture Garden / Ralph Cornell / Los Angeles, California, United States

Lake Elizabeth, Allegheny Commons / John Ormsbee Simonds / Pittsburgh, Pennsylvania, United States

Parc André Malraux / Jacques Sgard / Nanterre, France

▸ Milton Keynes in England formally designated as a new town.
▸ Artist Robert Smithson created his tour "Monuments of Passaic" in New Jersey.

**1968** **Jefferson National Expansion Memorial | Eero Saarinen, Dan Kiley | St. Louis, Missouri, United States**

Los Clubes / Luis Barragán / Mexico City, Mexico

Monument to the Negev Brigade / Dani Karavan / Beersheba, Israel

United States Air Force Academy / Dan Kiley / Colorado Springs, Colorado, United States

▸ "Earthrise" photographs taken by astronauts of the Apollo 8 mission.
▸ Charles and Ray Eames's *Powers of Ten* released.

**1969** **Oakland Museum of California | Dan Kiley | Oakland, California, United States**

Gulbenkian Park / Gonçalo Ribeiro Telles, António Viana Barreiro / Lisbon, Portugal

▸ Ian McHarg's *Design with Nature* published.
▸ Lawrence Halprin's *The RSVP Cycles: Creative Processes in the Human Environment* published.

**1970** **Spiral Jetty | Robert Smithson | Rozel Point, Utah, United States**

Botanic Garden, Arboretum of Mendelově University / Igor Otruba / Brno, Czech Republic

Copacabana Beach / Roberto Burle Marx / Rio de Janeiro, Brazil

*Double Negative* / Michael Heizer / Overton, Nevada, United States

Ira Keller Fountain / Lawrence Halprin / Portland, Oregon, United States

▸ Environmental Protection Agency (EPA) formed in the United States.
▸ First Earth Day celebration held in the United States.
▸ Nan Fairbrother's *New Lives, New Landscapes* published.

**1971** **Tucson Community Center | Garrett Eckbo | Tucson, Arizona, United States**

*Broken Circle/Spiral Hill* / Robert Smithson / Emmen, Netherlands

Greenacre Park / Hideo Sasaki / New York City, United States

▸ Walt Disney World opened in Orlando, Florida.
▸ Gordon Cullen's *The Concise Townscape* published.
▸ Jan Gehl's *Life Between Buildings* published.
▸ Norman Newton's *Design on the Land: The Development of Landscape Architecture* published.

**1972** **Olympiapark München | Behnisch & Partner, Günther Grzimek | Munich, Germany**

Chicago Botanic Garden / John Ormsbee Simonds et al. / Glencoe, Illinois, United States

Embarcadero–Justin Herman Plaza / Lawrence Halprin / San Francisco, California, United States

Water Garden / Lawrence Halprin / Olympia, Washington, United States

▸ Robert Venturi, Denise Scott Brown, and Steven Izenour's *Learning from Las Vegas* published.
▸ The United Nations Conference on the Human Environment held in Stockholm.
▸ United States government passed Clean Water Act.

**1973** **Jardin Zen | Erik Borja | Beaumont-Monteux, France**

Fukuchi-in Garden / Mirei Shigemori / Mount Kōya, Japan

Hallidie Plaza / Lawrence Halprin / San Francisco, California, United States

Liz Christy Garden / Elizabeth Christy / New York City, United States

**1974** **Fort Worth Water Gardens | Johnson/Burgee | Fort Worth, Texas, United States**

Parc des Coudrays / Michel Corajoud / Yvelines, France

Point State Park / Ralph E. Griswold, Charles M. Stotz / Pittsburgh, Pennsylvania, United States

Sarah Kubitschek Park / Roberto Burle Marx / Brasilia, Brazil

▶ Robert Caro's *The Power Broker: Robert Moses and the Fall of New York* published.

**1975** **Gas Works Park | Richard Haag | Seattle, Washington, United States**

Les Quatre Vents / Frank Cabot / Quebec, Canada

Matsuo Taisha Garden / Mirei Shigemori / Kyoto, Japan

Myodo Kyo Kai / Robert Murase / Shiga Prefecture, Japan

Peavey Plaza / M. Paul Friedberg / Minneapolis, Minnesota, United States

▶ Geoffrey Jellicoe and Susan Jellicoe's *The Landscape of Man: Shaping the Environment from Prehistory to the Present Day* published.
▶ Jay Appleton's *The Experience of Landscape* published.
▶ Project for Public Spaces founded in New York.

**1976** **Freeway Park | Lawrence Halprin | Seattle, Washington, United States**

Franklin Court / VSBA / Philadelphia, Pennsylvania, United States

Governor Nelson A. Rockefeller Empire State Plaza / Harrison & Abramovitz / Albany, New York, United States

Rock Garden / Nek Chand / Chandigarh, India

*Streams, Oberlin* / Athena Tacha / Hamilton, New Jersey, United States

▶ Charles Ross started *Star Axis* project in New Mexico.
▶ First United Nations Conference on Human Settlements (Habitat I) convened in Vancouver.

**1977** ***Observatorium* | Robert Morris | Lelystad, Netherlands**

Frick Garden / Russell Page / New York City, United States

Garden Bridge / Hans Luz / Stuttgart, Germany

*The Lightning Field* / Walter De Maria / Quemado, New Mexico, United States

▶ Christopher Alexander's *A Pattern Language: Towns, Buildings, Construction* published.

**1978** **Piazza d'Italia | Charles Moore | New Orleans, Louisiana, United States**

Brion-Vega Cemetery | Carlo Scarpa | San Vito d'Altivole, Italy (*100 Years, 100 Buildings*)

*Stone Enclosure: Rock Rings* / Nancy Holt / Bellingham, Washington, United States

*Time Landscape* / Alan Sonfist / New York City, United States

Waterfall Garden / Masao Kinoshita / Seattle, Washington, United States

▶ The American Planning Association formed.
▶ Colin Rowe's *Collage City* published.

**1979** **Robson Square | Cornelia Hahn Oberlander | Vancouver, British Columbia, Canada**

John F. Collins Park / John Francis Collins / Philadelphia, Pennsylvania, United States

Riverbank Park / Lawrence Halprin / Flint, Michigan, United States

Washington Federal Reserve Garden / Oehme van Sweden / Washington, DC, United States

▶ Artist James Turrell started *Roden Crater* project in New Mexico.

**1980** **Alexandra Road Park | Janet Jack | London, England**

Barbara Hepworth Museum and Sculpture Garden / Barbara Hepworth / St. Ives, England

Freedom Plaza / VSBA, George Patton / Washington, DC, United States

Heritage Park Plaza / Lawrence Halprin / Fort Worth, Texas, United States

▶ Claude Monet's garden at Giverny, France, opened to the public.
▶ Luis Barragán awarded the Pritzker Architecture Prize.
▶ William H. Whyte's *The Social Life of Small Urban Spaces* published.

**1981** **Seaside | Andres Duany, Elizabeth Plater-Zyberk | Seaside, Florida, United States**

Parc Départemental du Sausset / Claire Corajoud, Michel Corajoud / Aulnay-sous-Bois, France

Pershing Park / M. Paul Friedberg / Washington, DC, United States

▶ François Mitterrand began his *Grands Projets* in Paris.
▶ Richard Serra's *Tilted Arc* installed in Lower Manhattan.
▶ Team X dissolved.

**1982** **Vietnam Veterans Memorial | Maya Lin | Washington, DC, United States**

Barbican Water Gardens / Chamberlin, Powell and Bon / London, England

California Scenario / Isamu Noguchi / Costa Mesa, California, United States

Hummelo / Piet Oudolf / Hummelo, Netherlands

Plaza Italia / Miguel Angel Roca / Cordoba, Argentina

▶ Competition held in Paris for Parc de la Villette.

**1983** **Geometric Gardens | Carl Theodor Sørensen | Birk, Denmark**

Parc de Joan Miró / Beth Galí / Barcelona, Spain

Victor Steinbrueck Park / Richard Haag / Seattle, Washington, United States

Westpark / Peter Kluska, Rosemarie Weisse / Munich, Germany

▸ Christo and Jeanne-Claude's *Surrounded Islands* installed in Biscayne Bay, Miami, Florida.

▸ Darwina Neal became the first woman president of the American Society of Landscape Architects.

▸ First issue of *Places Journal* published.

**1984** **Tanner Fountain | Peter Walker | Cambridge, Massachusetts, United States**

All People's Trail / Schmidt Copeland / Shaker Heights, Ohio, United States

Pioneer Courthouse Square / Willard K. Martin / Portland, Oregon, United States

**1985** **Donald M. Kendall Sculpture Gardens | Edward Durell Stone Jr., Russell Page | Purchase, New York, United States**

16th Street Transitway Mall / Laurie Olin / Denver, Colorado, United States

Fountain Place / Dan Kiley / Dallas, Texas, United States

Jardins de Séricourt / Yves Gosse de Gorre / Séricourt, France

Parc de l'Espanya Industrial / Luis Peña Ganchegui / Barcelona, Spain

▸ Anne Whiston Spirn's *The Granite Garden: Urban Nature and Human Design* published.

**1986** **Bloedel Reserve Gardens | Richard Haag | Bainbridge Island, Washington, United States**

Crosby Arboretum / Edward L. Blake Jr. / Picayune, Mississippi, United States

Culiacán Botanical Garden / Carlos Murillo Depraect / Culiacán, Mexico

Leonhardt Lagoon Nature Walk / Patricia Johanson / Dallas, Texas, United States

Plaza del Tenis / Luis Peña Ganchegui, Eduardo Chillida / San Sebastián, Spain

**1987** **Parc de la Villette | Bernard Tschumi | Paris, France**

Ronneby Brunnspark / Sven-Ingvar Andersson / Ronneby, Sweden

**1988** ***Kikar Levana* | Dani Karavan | Tel Aviv, Israel**

Culhuacan Historical Park / Mario Schjetnan / Mexico City, Mexico

Kiley Garden / Dan Kiley / Tampa, Florida, United States

Minneapolis Sculpture Garden / Edward Larrabee Barnes, Peter Rothschild / Minneapolis, Minnesota, United States

South Cove / Susan Child, Mary Miss, Douglas Reed / New York City, United States

▸ Denatured Visions: Landscape and Culture in the Twentieth Century symposium held at the Museum of Modern Art, New York.

▸ Docomomo International founded in the Netherlands.

▸ Patrick Blanc installed his first vertical garden.

**1989** **Canadian Centre for Architecture Garden | Melvin Charney | Montreal, Canada**

New Parliament House / Peter Rolland / Canberra, Australia

Place Stalingrad / Bernard Huet / Paris, France

Plaza de Carlos III el Noble / Francisco Mangado Beloqui / Olite, Spain

Sherover Promenade / Shlomo Aronson / Jerusalem, Israel

▸ The Berlin Wall came down.

▸ The Garden Conservancy founded in New York.

▸ Loma Prieta earthquake struck San Francisco area.

**1990** **Jardín de Cactus | César Manrique | Guatiza, Lanzarote, Spain**

Guadalupe River Park / George Hargreaves / San Jose, California, United States

Monument to Sandro Pertini / Aldo Rossi / Milan, Italy

Shute House / Geoffrey Jellicoe / Shaftesbury, Dorset, England

Veddw House Garden / Anne Wareham / Devauden, Wales

▸ Ian McHarg became first landscape architect to receive U.S. National Medal of Art.

▸ Michael P. Conzen's *The Making of the American Landscape* published.

**1991** **Bryant Park | Laurie Olin | New York City, United States**

Biscayne Boulevard / Roberto Burle Marx / Miami, Florida, United States

Gibbs Farm / Noel Lane / Kaipara Harbor, New Zealand

University of Cincinnati / George Hargreaves / Cincinnati, Ohio, United States

▸ *Roberto Burle Marx: The Unnatural Art of the Garden* exhibition held at the Museum of Modern Art, New York.

**1992** **Parc André Citroën | Alain Provost, Gilles Clément | Paris, France**

Albert Promenade / Tichnun Nof / Mitzpe Ramon, Israel

Irish Sky Garden Crater / James Turrell / Skibbereen, Ireland

LongHouse Reserve / Jack Lenor Larsen / East Hampton, New York, United States

Valley of the Destroyed Communities, Yad Vashem /
Lipa Yahalom and Dan Zur / Jerusalem, Israel

▸ Barcelona hosted the Summer Olympics.

▸ Euro Disney opened in Paris.

▸ *Topos* – The International Review of Landscape Architecture and Urban Design founded.

## 1993 Parque Ecológico Xochimilco | Mario Schjetnan | Mexico City, Mexico

Promenade Plantée / Jacques Vergely, Philippe Mathieux, Patrick Berger / Paris, France

Swimming Pool El Guincho / Artengo Menis Pastrana / Adeje, Tenerife, Spain

Way of Human Rights / Dani Karavan / Nuremberg, Germany

▸ Congress for New Urbanism founded.

▸ Construction began on new town of Poundbury in England.

▸ *Modern Landscape Architecture: A Critical Review*, edited by Marc Treib, published.

## 1994 Igualada Cemetery | Enric Miralles, Carme Pinós | Igualada, Spain

Kreitman Plaza, Ben-Gurion University / Shlomo Aronson / Beersheba, Israel

Place des Terreaux / Christian Drevet / Lyon, France

Village of Yorkville Park / Martha Schwartz, Ken Smith, Peter Walker / Toronto, Ontario, Canada

▸ The Center for Land Use Interpretation founded in California.

▸ Norway started its National Tourist Routes project.

▸ Stockholm's Skogskyrkogården added to UNESCO World Heritage List.

## 1995 Site of Reversible Destiny—Yoro Park | Arakawa and Madeline Gins | Yoro, Japan

Fremont Street Experience / Jon Jerde / Las Vegas, Nevada, United States

Santo Domingo de Bonaval Park / Isabel Aguirre, Álvaro Siza / Santiago de Compostela, Spain

Swarovski Kristallwelten / André Heller / Wattens, Austria

▸ First issue of *Kerb: Journal of Landscape Architecture* published in Melbourne.

▸ Mathis Wackernagel and William E. Rees's *Our Ecological Footprint: Reducing Human Impact on the Earth* published.

## 1996 Les Jardins de l'Imaginaire | Kathryn Gustafson | Terrasson-Lavilledieu, France

Cedar Lake Park and Trail / Jones & Jones / Minneapolis, Minnesota, United States

The Green Cathedral / Marinus Boezem / Almere, Netherlands

Greenwood Pond: Double Site / Mary Miss / Des Moines, Iowa, United States

▸ Second United Nations Conference on Human Settlements (Habitat II) convened in Istanbul.

## 1997 *Central Garden* | Robert Irwin | Los Angeles, California, United States

*Desert Breath* / D.A.S.T. Arteam / El Gouna, Egypt

Franklin Delano Roosevelt Memorial / Lawrence Halprin / Washington, DC, United States

Invalidenpark / Christophe Girot, Atelier Phusis / Berlin, Germany

Schouwburgplein / West 8 / Rotterdam, Netherlands

▸ The Foundation for Landscape Studies established in New York.

▸ Landscape Urbanism conference held in Chicago.

▸ Martha Schwartz's Jacob Javits Plaza, the replacement for Richard Serra's *Tilted Arc*, opened in Lower Manhattan.

## 1998 Il Giardino dei Tarocchi | Niki de Saint Phalle | Garavicchio, Italy

Cemetery of the Unknown / Hideki Yoshimatsu, Archipro Architects / Hiroshima, Japan

Crazannes Quarries / Bernard Lassus / Saintes-Rochefort, France

Hotel Le Port Kojimachi / Shunmyo Masuno / Tokyo, Japan

HUD Plaza / Martha Schwartz / Washington, DC, United States

▸ The Cultural Landscape Foundation (TCLF) established.

▸ First International Biennale of Landscape Architecture held in Barcelona.

▸ *The Truman Show*, filmed in Seaside, Florida, released.

## 1999 Jardí Botànic de Barcelona | Carlos Ferrater, Josep Lluís Canosa, Bet Figueras | Barcelona, Spain

Exchange Square / Martha Schwartz / Manchester, England

Fisterra Cemetery / César Portela Fernandez-Jardón / Fisterra, Spain

Mile End Park / Piers Gough / London, England

Scampston Walled Garden / Piet Oudolf / Malton, England

▸ The European Prize for Urban Public Space established in Barcelona.

▸ Friends of the High Line formed in New York.

## 2000 La Granja Escalators | José Antonio Martínez Lapeña, Elías Torres Tur | Toledo, Spain

Four Vigas / Solano Benitez / Piribebuy, Paraguay

Sydney Olympic Millennium Parklands / Peter Walker / Sydney, Australia

Thames Barrier Park / Alain Provost / London, England

▸ European Landscape Convention adopted.

▸ First International Garden Festival held at Reford Gardens in Quebec.

▸ SketchUp 3D software released.

**2001**  Landschaftspark Duisburg-Nord | Latz + Partner | Duisburg, Germany

Crissy Field / Hargreaves Associates / San Francisco, California, United States

Desert Plaza / Eduardo Arroyo / Barakaldo, Spain

Parterre du Carrousel, Tuileries / Jacques Wirtz / Paris, France

▸ Eden Project opened to the public in Cornwall, England.

▸ Elizabeth Barlow Rogers's *Landscape Design: A Cultural and Architectural History* published.

▸ Competition for former Fresh Kills Landfill in New York City held.

**2002**  MFO-Park | Burckhardt+Partner, Raderschall Partner | Zürich, Switzerland

Jardin Botanique de Bordeaux / Catherine Mosbach / La Bastide, France

Landform Ueda / Charles Jencks / Edinburgh, Scotland

Federation Square / Karres+Brands / Melbourne, Australia

Zhongshan Shipyard Park / Turenscape / Guangdong, China

**2003**  Parque da Juventude | aflalo / gasperini, Rosa Kliass | São Paulo, Brazil

Líthica / Laetitia Lara, José Bravo / Menorca, Spain

Garraf Waste Landfill / Batlle i Roig / Spain

Nasher Sculpture Center Garden / Peter Walker / Dallas, Texas, United States

Tokachi Millennium Forest / Dan Pearson / Hokkaido, Japan

▸ Robert Thayer's *LifePlace: Bioregional Thought and Practice* published.

**2004**  Millennium Park | Skidmore, Owings & Merrill | Chicago, Illinois, United States

Beck Park / Mesa Design Group / Dallas, Texas, United States

Diana, Princess of Wales Memorial Fountain / Gustafson Porter / London, England

Forum Southeast Coastal Park / FOA / Barcelona, Spain

Teardrop Park / Michael Van Valkenburgh / New York City, United States

**2005**  Cheonggyecheon River Park | SeoAhn Total Landscape | Seoul, South Korea

Atlanta BeltLine / Ryan Gravel / Atlanta, Georgia, United States

Memorial to the Murdered Jews of Europe / Peter Eisenman / Berlin, Germany

Ring Walk / Durbach Block / Sydney, Australia

Termas Geométricas / Germán del Sol / Coñaripe, Chile

▸ Christo and Jeanne-Claude's *The Gates* installed in New York's Central Park.

▸ First "Edible Estate" planted by artist Fritz Haeg, in Salina, Kansas.

▸ *Groundswell: Constructing the Contemporary Landscape* exhibition held at the Museum of Modern Art, New York.

**2006**  Australian Garden, Royal Botanic Gardens | Taylor Cullity Lethlean | Cranbourne, Australia

Buffalo Bayou Park / SWA / Houston, Texas, United States

Instituto Inhotim / Roberto Burle Marx, Pedro Nehring, Luiz Carlos Orsini / Brumadinho, Brazil

Musée de Quai Branly / Gilles Clément, Patrick Blanc / Paris, France

Renaissance Park / George Hargreaves / Chattanooga, Tennessee, United States

▸ Arup unveiled plan for Dongtan Eco-City near Shanghai.

▸ Charles Waldheim's *The Landscape Urbanism Reader* published.

▸ Patrick Taylor's *The Oxford Companion to the Garden* published.

**2007**  Olympic Sculpture Park | Weiss/Manfredi | Seattle, Washington, United States

General Maister Memorial Park / Bruto / Ljubno ob Savinji, Slovenia

HTO Park / Janet Rosenberg, Claude Cormier / Toronto, Ontario, Canada

Jinhua Architecture Park / Ai Weiwei / Jinhua City, China

▸ Alan Berger's *Drosscape: Wrestling Land in Urban America* published.

▸ The global population of people in cities surpassed people in rural areas for the first time.

**2008**  Qinhuangdao Red Ribbon Park | Turenscape | Qinhuangdao, China

Forest Walk / LOOK Architects / Singapore

Rose Fitzgerald Kennedy Greenway / Perkins + Will / Boston, Massachusetts, United States

Vancouver Land Bridge / Jones & Jones / Vancouver, British Columbia, Canada

Vache Noire / Agence Ter / Arcueil, France

▸ Olafur Eliasson installed *The New York City Waterfalls* under the Brooklyn Bridge.

**2009**  Orpheus at Boughton | Kim Wilkie | Kettering, England

Barry Curtis Park / Isthmus Group / Manukau City, New Zealand

Benidorm Waterfront / Carlos Ferrater / Barcelona, Spain

Pedestrian Bridge over Carpinteira River /

João Luís Carrilho da Graçã / Covilhá, Portugal

South Pointe Park / George Hargreaves / Miami, Florida, United States

▸ Ecological Urbanism conference held at Harvard University.

▸ Exhibition on Roberto Burle Marx held at Paço Imperial in Rio de Janeiro.

▸ *In Situ: Architecture and Landscape* exhibition held at the Museum of Modern Art, New York.

## 2010 Moses Bridge | RO&AD Architecten | Halsteren, Netherlands

The City Dune, SEB Bank / Stig L. Andersson / Copenhagen, Denmark

Evergreen Brick Works / Claude Cormier / Toronto, Ontario, Canada

Nature Boardwalk at Lincoln Park Zoo / Studio Gang / Chicago, Illinois, United States

Shanghai Houtan Park / Turenscape / Shanghai, China

▸ Enzo Enea opened the Tree Museum in Rapperswil-Jona, Switzerland.

▸ Martha Schwartz's Jacob Javits Plaza removed in Lower Manhattan.

▸ *Rising Currents: Projects for New York's Waterfront* exhibition held at the Museum of Modern Art, New York.

## 2011 Madrid Río | MRIO Arquitectos, West 8 | Madrid, Spain

La Lira / RCR Arquitectes / Ripoll, Spain

Metropol Parasol | J. Mayer H. | Seville, Spain (*100 Years, 100 Buildings*)

National September 11 Memorial / Michael Arad, Peter Walker / New York City, United States

▸ Earthquake and tsunami strike off the coast of Japan.

## 2012 Bay South, Gardens by the Bay | Grant Associates | Singapore

Franklin D. Roosevelt Four Freedoms Park / Louis I. Kahn / New York City, United States

New Government City / Diana Balmori / Seoul, South Korea

Queen Elizabeth Olympic Park / Hargreaves Associates, LDA Design / London, England

Superkilen / Topotek 1, BIG Architects, Superflex / Copenhagen, Denmark

▸ Digital Landscape Now symposium held at Harvard University.

▸ London hosted the Summer Olympics.

▸ Lower Manattan lost power when Superstorm Sandy hit the northeastern United States.

## 2013 Parco Portello | Charles Jencks, Andreas Kipar | Milan, Italy

The Braided Valley / Francisco Leiva Ivorra et al. / Elche, Spain

Hunter's Point South Waterfront Park / Thomas Balsley Associates and Weiss/Manfredi / New York City, United States

Rénovation du Vieux-Port / Michel Desvigne et al. / Marseille, France

## 2014 High Line | James Corner Field Operations, Diller Scofidio + Renfro, Piet Oudolf | New York City, United States

The Clark / Reed Hilderbrand / Williamstown, Massachusetts, United States

Qingdao Expo / HHD_FUN / Qingdao, China

Taekwondo Park / Weiss/Manfredi / Muju, South Korea

Yanweizhou Park / Turenscape / Jinhua City, China

## 2015 *Grande Cretto* | Alberto Burri | Gibellina, Sicily, Italy

The Goods Line / ASPECT Studios / Sydney, Australia

La Misteriosa Historia del Jardín Que Produce Agua / Cómo Crear Historias / Murcia, Spain

Renaturation of the River Aire / Georges Descombes / Geneva, Switzerland

Sydney Park Water Re-Use Project / Turf Design Studio / Sydney, Australia

## 2016 The Park | !melk | Las Vegas, Nevada, United States

Chicago Riverwalk / Sasaki Associates, Ross Barney Architects / Chicago, Illinois, United States

Governors Island / West 8 et al. / New York City, United States

Jardins de la Rambla de Sants / Sergi Godia, Ana Molino / Barcelona, Spain

▸ Christo's *The Floating Piers* installed on Lake Iseo, Italy.

▸ The New Landscape Declaration: A Summit on Landscape Architecture and the Future held in Philadelphia.

▸ Third United Nations Conference on Human Settlements (Habitat III) convened in Quito.

# GENERAL BIBLIOGRAPHY

Abascal, Jimena Blázquez. *Sculpture Parks in Europe: A Guide to Art and Nature.* Basel, Switzerland: Birkhäuser, 2002.

Adams, William Howard. *Grounds for Change: Major Gardens of the Twentieth Century.* Boston: Bulfinch Press, 1993.

Arpa, Javier, and Aurora Fernández Per. *The Public Chance: New Urban Landscapes.* Vitoria-Gasteiz, Spain: a+t ediciones, 2008.

Berner, Nancy, and Susan Lowry. *Garden Guide: New York City.* Rev. ed. New York: W. W. Norton, 2010.

Birnbaum, Charles A., and Robin S. Karson. *Pioneers of American Landscape Design.* New York: McGraw Hill, 2000.

Birnbaum, Charles A., and Stephanie S. Foell. *Shaping the American Landscape: New Profiles from the Pioneers of American Landscape Design Project.* Charlottesville: University of Virginia Press, 2009.

Brown, Jane. *The Modern Garden.* New York: Princeton Architectural Press, 2000.

Campbell, Katie. *Icons of Twentieth-Century Landscape Design.* London: Frances Lincoln, 2006.

Chappell, Sally A. Kitt. *Chicago's Urban Nature: A Guide to the City's Architecture and Landscape.* Chicago: University of Chicago Press, 2007.

Cohen, Susan. *The Inspired Landscape: Twenty-One Leading Landscape Architects Explore the Creative Process.* Portland, OR: Timber Press, 2015.

Cooper, Guy. *Gardens for the Future: Gestures against the Wild.* New York: Monacelli Press, 2000.

Corner, James. *Recovering Landscape: Essays in Contemporary Landscape Architecture.* New York: Princeton Architectural Press, 1999.

De Poli, Michela, and Guido Incerti. *An Atlas of Recycled Landscapes.* Milan: Skira, 2014.

Foy, George, and Sidney Lawrence. *Music in Stone: Great Sculpture Gardens of the World.* New York: Scala Books, 1984.

*The Garden Book.* London: Phaidon, 2005.

Hunt, John Dixon. *The Making of Place: Modern and Contemporary Gardens.* London: Reaktion Books, 2015.

Jellicoe, Geoffrey, and Susan Jellicoe. *The Landscape of Man: Shaping the Environment from Prehistory to the Present Day.* 3rd ed. London: Thames and Hudson, 1995.

Johnson, Jory. *Modern Landscape Architecture: Redefining the Garden.* New York: Abbeville Press, 1991.

Kassler, Elizabeth B. *Modern Gardens and the Landscape.* New York: Museum of Modern Art, 1964.

Kastner, Jeffrey. *Land and Environmental Art.* London: Phaidon, 2010.

Reed, Peter. *Groundswell: Constructing the Contemporary Landscape.* New York: Museum of Modern Art, 2005.

Rogers, Elizabeth Barlow. *Landscape Design: A Cultural and Architectural History.* New York: Harry N. Abrams, 2001.

Ryan, Raymund. *White Cube, Green Maze: New Art Landscapes.* Berkeley: University of California Press, 2012.

Simo, Melanie Louise. *100 Years of Landscape Architecture: Some Patterns of a Century.* Washington, DC: ASLA Press, 1999.

Tate, Alan. *Great City Parks.* 2nd ed. London: Routledge, 2015.

Taylor, Kristina. *Women Garden Designers: 1900 to the Present.* Woodbridge, England: Garden Art Press, 2015.

Taylor, Patrick. *The Oxford Companion to the Garden.* Oxford: Oxford University Press, 2006.

Thompson, Ian H. *Landscape Architecture: A Very Short Introduction.* Oxford: Oxford University Press, 2014.

Tilden, Scott J. *The Glory of Gardens: 2,000 Years of Writings on Garden Design.* New York: Harry N. Abrams, 2006.

Treib, Marc. *Modern Landscape Architecture: A Critical Review.* Cambridge, MA: MIT Press, 1994.

———. *The Architecture of Landscape, 1940–1960.* Philadelphia: University of Pennsylvania Press, 2002.

Tunnard, Christopher. *Gardens in the Modern Landscape: A Facsimile of the Revised 1948 Edition.* Philadelphia: University of Pennsylvania Press, 2014.

Walker, Peter, and Melanie Simo. *Invisible Gardens: The Search for Modernism in the American Landscape.* Cambridge, MA: MIT Press, 1994.

Waterman, Tim. *The Fundamentals of Landscape Architecture.* 2nd ed. London: Bloomsbury, 2015.

Waymark, Janet. *Modern Garden Design: Innovation Since 1900.* London: Thames and Hudson, 2003.

# ACKNOWLEDGMENTS

First I want to thank Robin Key and Gareth Mahon of Robin Key Landscape Architecture (RKLA), whose input, expertise, and resources were invaluable in the preliminary and research stages of this book. It was Gareth who first mentioned I should write a landscape version of *100 Years, 100 Buildings*; without his prompting I might not have considered it.

A big thanks to Holly La Due at Prestel, editor on my previous book, for agreeing to make another go of the one-hundred-years format. Her input on the projects and photographs during the making of the book made it that much better.

I have to admit the appeal of books about landscapes stems in large part from great photos. So thanks to Emma Gunuey and, especially, Sophie Golub for their hard work in the often-frustrating task of finding photographs, obtaining permissions, and dealing with an at-times disagreeable author. Thanks to the institutions and landscape architecture firms who contributed photos. And thanks to the photographers I'm indebted to for their generosity: Alessandra Chemollo, Leonardo Finotti, Christopher Karlson, Ken McCown, Trevor Patt, Dan Pearson, Brigitte Rieser, Daniel Roush, and Victor Tsu.

Thanks to my family, especially my mum, Eileen, whose love of gardening must have rubbed off on me somewhere along the way. Lastly thanks, as always, to my wife, Karen, and my daughter, Clare, for indulging me in yet another one of my passions.

# PHOTOGRAPHY CREDITS

© Prestel Verlag, Munich · London · New York 2017
A member of Verlagsgruppe Random House GmbH
Neumarkter Strasse 28 · 81673 Munich

In respect to links in the book, Verlagsgruppe Random House expressly notes that no illegal content was discernible on the linked sites at the time the links were created. The Publisher has no influence at all over the current and future design, content or authorship of the linked sites. For this reason Verlagsgruppe Random House expressly disassociates itself from all content on linked sites that has been altered since the link was created and assumes no liability for such content.

Text © 2017 John Hill

Prestel Publishing Ltd.
14-17 Wells Street
London W1T 3PD

Prestel Publishing
900 Broadway, Suite 603
New York, NY 10003

Library of Congress Cataloging-in-Publication Control Number: 2017011978

A CIP catalogue record for this book is available from the British Library.

Editorial direction: Holly La Due
Editorial assistance: Sophie Golub
Design and layout: Laura Lindgren Design
Production management: Luke Chase
Copyediting: Kara Pickman
Proofreading: Kelli Rae Patton

Case binding: Jardí Botánic de Barcelona
by Carlos Ferrater, Josep Lluís Canosa, and
Bet Figueras, Barcelona, Spain

Pages 2–3, 98–99: View of the South Fields, all works by Mark di Suvero, born China, 1933. *Pyramidian*, 1987/1988. *Beethoven's Quartet*, 2003, Courtesy Tippet Rise Art Center; *Mon Père, Mon Père*, 1973–75. *Mother Peace*, 1969–70. Except where noted, all works Gift of the Ralph E. Ogden Foundation, Inc.

Pages 4–5: Spiral Jetty by Robert Smithson, Rozel Point, Utah, United States (see p. 118)

Page 6: The High Line by James Corner Field Operations, Diller Scofidio + Renfro, Piet Oudolf, New York City, United States (see p. 206)

Verlagsgruppe Random House FSC® N001967
Printed on the FSC®-certified paper
NEO matt art

ISBN 978-3-7913-8310-1

www.prestel.com